A1128

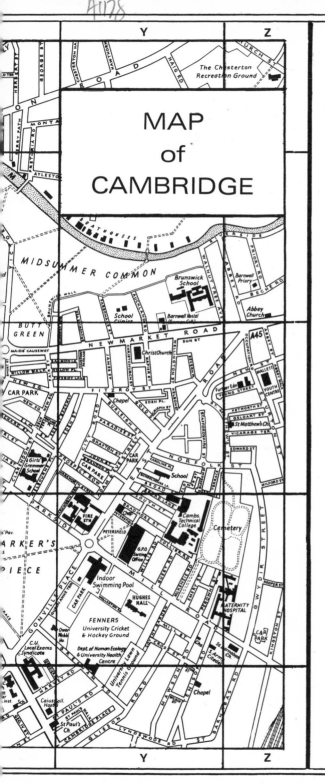

MAP
of
CAMBRIDGE

C000183905

Colleg...

College		Map Square
Caius		
Christ...		
Church...		
Clare		
Corpus Christi	DW	43
Darwin	DV	96
Downing	DX	85
Emmanuel	CX	79
Fitzwilliam	AU	90
Girton *Off Map See*	AV	85
Gonville and Caius	CW	37
Jesus	BX	57
King's	CW	47
Magdalene	BW	71
New Hall	AV	87
Newnham	DV	86
Pembroke	DW	33
Peterhouse	DW	25
Queens'	DW	51
Saint Catherine's	DW	55
Saint John's	CW	67
Selwyn	DU	85
Sidney Sussex	CW	80
Trinity	CW	74
Trinity Hall	CW	41

Other Buildings

	Map Square
Great Saint Mary's Church	CW
Saint Benet's Church	DW
Senate House	CW
University Centre	DW
University Library	CV

Map of Cambridge by kind permission of
Heffers of Cambridge.

*Based upon the Ordnance Survey Map with the sanction of the
Controller of H.M. Stationery Office Crown Copyright reserved*

THE UNIVERSITY AND COLLEGES OF CAMBRIDGE

Other Books by Rodney Tibbs:

Fenland River
King's College Chapel, Cambridge

THE UNIVERSITY AND COLLEGES
OF CAMBRIDGE

by

RODNEY TIBBS

TERENCE DALTON LIMITED
LAVENHAM . SUFFOLK
1972

Published by
TERENCE DALTON LIMITED
SBN 900963 38 7

First impression 1972

Second impression 1975

Printed in Great Britain at

THE LAVENHAM PRESS LIMITED

LAVENHAM   SUFFOLK

To Annie

CONTENTS

INDEX OF ILLUSTRATIONS

FOREWORD AND ACKNOWLEDGEMENT

TO WRITE a book about the University and colleges of Cambridge means defining one's objectives from the very start, and a quick glance at the many volumes which have been devoted to the subject in the past will show that setting out the problem is much easier than finding a solution. Some works have furthered man's academic knowledge of this magnificent university city and the colleges and institutions within it. Others have contented themselves with merely assisting the visitor around its narrow and ancient streets with the minimum of delay and the maximum of enjoyment. Between these extremes come numerous and very worthy writers throughout the ages who have reminisced, discussed, instructed and recalled often with charming and illuminating results.

But Cambridge does not stand still, even though much of its glory was created in the past. Our present century has seen the foundation of more new colleges and potential colleges than at any time during the previous 200 years. The process is a continuous one, and as it goes along it offers a challenge to those with a leaning towards setting it all down in print in an effort to share their enjoyment with others.

And that is what this book is basically designed to do. Enjoyment for those who cannot visit Cambridge in person, enjoyment for those who do. I am hopeful that the story of the place will in itself provide the reader with a narrative which will carry him on from college to college, from chapter to chapter. This approach has its pitfalls but I am hopeful that most of them have been avoided and that the book will prove an entertaining and instructive companion for anyone wishing to know more about one of the most historically important and beautiful cities in the world.

Of course one cannot produce a book of this sort without the assistance of a considerable number of people. Fortunately there is something about Cambridge which compels those living and working within its influence to talk about it. We have become the beneficiaries. Mr James Claydon of the Cambridge University Library and his colleagues have again given much willing and valuable help. I am also particularly indebted to Miss Enid Porter of the Cambridge and County Folk Museum who must surely rank as one of the foremost authorities on Cambridge and its past. I must thank also Michael Petty, the curator of the Local Collection of Cambridge City Libraries, who has built up an immensely valuable collection of Cambridge material. Among my own colleagues at the Cambridge Evening News I must express my gratitude to Cedric Tarrant, the chief photographer, for offering much technical advice when my own technical knowledge ran thin, and to Dennis Long and his staff in the library for their willingness to put me on the right track from time to time.

Also behind this book are innumerable college servants, Fellows, gardeners and officials who have borne my intrusion and questioning with the same fortitude and patience that they annually display to a host of visitors.

Finally I would thank John Venmore-Rowland of Terence Dalton Limited for his usual expert advice and the artist Roger Finch for his gifted work for the dust jacket.

Rodney Tibbs,
Cambridge.

April 1972

Trinity Great Gate and fountain.

CHAPTER ONE

Cambridge, Town and University

CAMBRIDGE is unique. Of course this can be said of any place for no two
towns are exactly alike but at Cambridge the word takes on a more positive
meaning. With Oxford, Cambridge shares the distinction of being one of the two
oldest universities in this country, but unlike Oxford it has avoided industrial
overtones and preserves much of its original character as a quiet place of thought
on the edge of the Fens. It has always been a centre for scholars. Now it is a centre
for visitors as well. They come from all parts of the world to walk among its
narrow medieval streets, to study architecture of every period and of almost every
century, to inspect its many important literary and artistic treasures. They also
wander along "The Backs", that interlinking series of college gardens and grounds
to the west of the river which must surely represent the ultimate in town planning.
The Backs are what every architect and planner would like to achieve when he
sets out to create a new building or a new city. But it would seem that such a
balance of garden and building, of shape and form, of peace, quiet and constantly
changing scene is only achieved once in the world.

How did it all come about? What was the essential ingredient which turned
an otherwise ordinary market town into a place of such distinction, of such
history and of such beauty? Perhaps we shall never know. However, we can
answer such factual questions as to why Cambridge town came to be so placed at
its present bend in the river, and we know why it was to become the focal point
for scholars moving away from Oxford, but beyond that it is often difficult to go.
Cambridge town existed before the first arrival of teaching and learning and so we
may as well consider it first. In the days long before even the Romans it must
have been a vastly different place from today. To the immediate north were the
vast bogs and swamps of the undrained Fens. Much of it formed a large inland sea
which could only be negotiated by boat and then only by someone who knew
what he was doing. To the south the area was covered by impenetrable forests,
unpleasant places for the foot traveller, thick with undergrowth and scrub pro-
viding a hiding place for enemies, human as well as animal. In addition to these
natural hindrances to movement the traveller wishing to go from East Anglia to
the Midlands or vice versa found his path blocked at the lowest point of the inland
sea by a river. Fortunately there was a way through. A number of river valleys
met below this point which meant that the traveller only had to cross one stream,
the Cam. If he skirted round the bottom edge of the inland sea, which is represented today on a much smaller scale by The Wash, he found a chalk outcrop
which formed a boundary between the water and the edge of the forests. This
provided him with a reasonably sound path right up to the river and its ford.

The Senate House.

Once over this he could swing north, still travelling along the edge of the Fenland wet areas, or he could continue to the west.

It was at this point, where the river was fordable and there was clearly considerable strategic value, that a settlement formed which was later to become the Town of Cambridge.

There is some evidence that the Romans, with all their road building expertise, were not above improving the existing tracks they encountered, and it is my guess that long before Cambridge became an important Roman junction of cross routes it was an equally busy meeting point for even earlier trackways. A well preserved Iron Age settlement at Wandlebury* on the chalk outcrop to the south east of the town emphasises the strategic importance of the river crossing even before the Romans came. Today it is still possible to stand on the site of the Iron Age fort and enjoy a magnificent view of Cambridge on the lower ground astride the river. The skyline is punctuated by the pinnacles and towers of university and

*Wandlebury is now contained within a large country estate on the Gog Magog Hills bought by the Cambridge Preservation Society. It is open to the public.

St Benet's Church, the oldest in Cambridge. It was in this church that lectures were given to some of the first scholars.

Great St Mary's, the University Church.

town buildings. Take away the massive chimney and bulk of the new Addenbrooke's Hospital site and remove the blunt-nosed tower of the University Library and the place would look much as it did when the university and later the colleges were first established.

The Romans advanced from the east and their road is still beautifully preserved as it passes not far from Wandlebury. This is the Via Devana coming up from the great Roman settlement at Colchester, running through the centre of present day Cambridge and becoming the A.604 as it runs north to Huntingdon. There is evidence from such ancient waterways as Carr Dyke that the Romans had already begun to drain part of the Fens and good communications with the southern part of the drier area would have been necessary. This was probably provided by another of their roads, Akeman Street, which ran north eastwards from Ermine Street, crossed the Granta at Croydon, passed Cambridge and then went on to reach Ely by means of a raised causeway.

13

It was not long before the ford across the river had been replaced by a bridge, one of the earliest bridges in England and the only one to give a county town its name. Camford and Oxbridge? The names might have worked out that way if history had taken a slightly different course at this point. An entry in the Anglo-Saxon Chronicle under the year 875 giving the name Grantebryge not only shows that a bridge had replaced a ford by this time but it is also one of the earliest recorded uses of the word bridge. It may have been built during the reign of Offa (757–796) when the Kingdom of Mercia was at the height of its power. At the time of the Domesday Book in 1086, Cambridge had become a small town using the curve of the river on one side as its westerly defence and employing an artificial watercourse, The King's Ditch, to enclose it to the east.

It remains an important meeting point of almost exactly similar roads to this day. The diversity of the cattle, stock and various wares which were brought to its markets in the very early days also remains much the same because it still represents a meeting point, not only of roads, but of different geological underlying structures which have always had the effect of producing different types of farming within relatively short distances.

This much, as I have said, is fairly safe ground but if we turn to the origins of the University and later the colleges, opinion has been sharply divided for many years. Strong rivalry has grown up between Cambridge and Oxford in which scholars from both places have set out to prove that each was the older and that each came first. Professor Maitland addressing an Oxford audience once said, "The oldest of the inter-university sports was a lying match." It is a slightly cynical view but there is evidence to recommend it. In the contests of ingenuity in arriving at suitable explanations Cambridge does seem to have had some advantages. A Papal Bull from Honorius I dated 624 was put forward at one time as evidence that Cambridge came first although its appearance was considered highly convenient! I should explain that all universities at that time could only be created by the Pope although this did not become the general rule until after 1250.

It is now generally accepted, both in Cambridge and Oxford, that there were recognisable schools in Oxford in the year 1167 about forty years before they are heard of at Cambridge. Schools are not necessarily universities and schools of that period were inclined to appear and then die. Certainly those at Cambridge went through some difficult periods before they reached University status. A university has privileges of its own and a high degree of permanence. Oxford and Cambridge seemed to jog along quite well without bothering to integrate themselves into the family of European universities, also granted by the Pope, until outside pressures made it both sensible and adroit to do so. In the year 1209 there were definitely Clerks at Cambridge who had arrived from Oxford. Upheavals and antagonism at Oxford brought about by King John's hostility to the Clerks is believed to have

The University Library. The top of the tower provided an ideal lookout post for fire watchers.

been the cause of the easterly migration. But if Oxford had scholars who could leave it, Cambridge certainly had schools to which they could go — so we are not much closer to deciding which came first.

By 1231 Cambridge students were sufficient in numbers and apparently so unruly that Henry III issued a number of writs for the punishment of disorderly scholars by the Sheriff, for the expulsion of scholars who were not under the direction of a master, and for the regulation of their rents and lodgings. This was to be undertaken by two masters and "two good and lawful men of the town." The action taken by Henry throws a certain amount of light on life in Cambridge at that time. It is quite clear that the University had no buildings of its own to serve as schools for its classes or lodgings for its members. Lectures were given in houses hired from townspeople and in some cases were given in a church.

We know that the Church of St Benet was used for this purpose and that the University paid the Clerk for ringing the bell for summoning the scholars. Later scholars began to live in hostels sometimes run by townsfolk but mainly by a Master of Arts and this system flourished alongside the colleges for some time after they first began to appear. By the middle of the sixteenth century they were annexed or suppressed by the colleges. The word "hosteller" became "ostler", a term familiar in later years to the readers of Dickens and other writers of the great coaching period.

Cambridge University, as such, had still not obtained for itself official Papal recognition and was already having trouble with the Bishops of Ely who were decidedly jealous of the manner in which it appeared to be usurping some of their power and responsibilities. In 1318 the University got itself officially baptised with a Papal Bull from Pope John XXII raising it to a "Studium Generale" or University; Oxford got confirmation of its privileges from Pope Innocent IV in 1254 but it was never technically christened a University, a point not overlooked by Cambridge in the 'who came first' controversy!

Clearly both Oxford and Cambridge had been giving themselves the title 'University' for something like a century before they were officially entitled to it and it is reasonable to spend a few moments looking at the exact meaning of the word at the time. The name Universitas is very old and its application to scholastic corporations began with the first Italian Universities of Salerno and Bologna. In the twelfth century it became applied to any body of men who possessed a collective legal status and rights which could be legally enforced against individuals or other corporations. The Universitas could be a town, county or guild, A teaching Universitas was a guild of scholars not unlike a trade or craft guild in that it could make its own conditions of membership, laws for its government, fees for its members, and take steps to prevent outsiders from meddling in its affairs.

Trade guilds of the time usually had a hall for meetings, sometimes a chapel and one or more chaplains. They met for secular and religious purposes in a parish church. In the light of this it becomes understandable that the guild of scholars of Cambridge met at the Church of St Benet's and St Mary's. Even though there were such similarities between trade and scholastic guilds at the time there was one important and far-reaching difference. Trade guilds operated on a purely local scale with their members selling goods in the town in which they lived. The scholastic guild at Cambridge contained members from all parts of the country and its arms began to reach to the furthest corners of the British Isles.

In due course Oxford and Cambridge were to develop an influence which stretched not only through the United Kingdom but throughout the world. This however is a later, and more fascinating side of the story.

Rowing, and college boathouses, have long been a feature of the River Cam. The boathouse in the centre is a modern addition and is shared by Corpus Christi and Sidney Sussex colleges.

CHAPTER TWO

The Golden Years

EVEN in the thirteenth century the University was having problems of discipline. Students belonged to no particular body, were not responsible to any one person and came and went in an irregular manner. In 1276 we learn that, "no one shall receive a scholar who has not had a fixed master within fifteen days after the said scholar has entered the University." Here was the University, itself the only apparent semblance of system and order in a situation of fluidity and chaos, trying to establish some sort of pattern. If it was better that the student was attached to a "fixed master" surely it would be an even greater improvement if students were gathered together into some sort of community which enjoyed a form of corporate life. The Ordinance attaching a student to a master certainly had the special approval of Hugh de Balsham, Bishop of Ely from 1257 to 1286 and it was through him that a solution to the University's disciplinary problems was found in the inauguration of the college system. It is interesting that the medieval tradition of community life which was incorporated into the college system has remained in the English Universities although it has now almost disappeared from the Continent. Bishop Hugh took the first step towards a college structure almost unintentionally it seems. He placed some scholars in the Augustinian Hospital of St John at Cambridge but before long it was clear that discipline, rather than improving by bringing a group of scholars together as a body, had deteriorated through very poor relations with the Brethren.

The scholars were then moved to two houses next to the Church of St Peter outside Trumpington Gate on the Trumpington Road. To help with their maintenance they were assigned two houses and the Church, with its tithes and altar dues. There was still no attempt to form them into a college. They were known as "the scholars of the Bishop of Ely" and their Letters Patent were dated March 31st 1284. The house came to be known as "The House of St Peter" and Bishop Hugh died in June 1286. The earliest Statutes of his foundation were given to it by Simon Montagu, Bishop of Ely, round about the year 1338. Thus gradually and without conscious design the beginnings of the college system began to evolve, and Peterhouse, the first Cambridge college, was brought into being.

It was the only Cambridge college founded in the thirteenth century. The colleges which were to follow can become confusing to the modern visitor to the City because some do not bear the name they were originally given. As in today's hard world of commerce there were mergers and takeovers. Michaelhouse, founded by Hervey de Stanton in 1324, was a good example. De Stanton was Chancellor of the Exchequer at the time and established a college known as "The Scholars of

Garret Hostel Bridge spans a typical river scene on a summer's day. The bridge, built in 1960, is made of concrete and is of one arch 80 feet in span.

St Michael". This became Michaelhouse which was afterwards merged into the Trinity College of today.

The early part of the fourteenth century was rich in new foundations. In 1326 the University itself bought two houses and converted them into a house of learning, no doubt to celebrate the fact that it had at last got documents giving it official standing in the eyes of Pope John XXII. It had every reason to be gleeful. The rights it had obtained made it independent of the Bishop of the Diocese and supreme power was given to the head of the University, the Chancellor.

The name of this college was University Hall and it had only a twelve year existence before it was re-endowed and rebuilt by Elizabeth de Burgh, Countess of Clare, in whose honour it took its present name of Clare College.

In the meantime Edward III seemed to be engaged in college founding although he did not arrive on the scene with any great fanfare of trumpets and suitable pomp and circumstance. The documents which survive allow us to become dimly aware that he was maintaining children at Cambridge who were placed there by his father, Edward II. A fragmentary writ which remains tells us John de Baggeshote "and twelve other children of his chapel at the University of Cambridge" were to receive money from the Sheriff of Cambridgeshire for their food, rent of their hostel and other necessities.

One of the problems of probing into the early beginnings of such institutions as colleges is that just about all the information which comes down to us is in the form of documents preserved by college libraries and other bodies. Often the contents are dry but occasionally, and Edward II's foundation is a good example, the real colour of life in those days breaks through. The children he had established at Cambridge at King's Hall reached the total of thirty-two by 1319. We know that on December 7th of that year they were ordered to spend Christmas with the Court at York. Six of the scholars left Cambridge on horseback in the care of the Warden and the remainder went most of the way by boat. One party was back in Cambridge by January 20th after a suitably festive season at Court and the other turned up on February 9th. At least one scholar remained in York having been arrested for assault!

In 1326 Edward II gave his scholars law books which were promptly taken away from them by his Queen, Isabella. Ten pounds was subsequently paid to them in compensation by Edward III in 1332. Clearly the scholastic life of those days had its own little ups and downs.

Eventually, as in the case of Michaelhouse, Henry VIII absorbed King's Hall into the college which survives today, Trinity, one which has given its name to Trinity Street and was attended by Prince Charles in 1968. Pembroke College was founded in 1347 by the wife of the Earl of Pembroke and Pembroke College it remains today. The following year Edmund Gonville, Rector of Terrington in Norfolk, founded a college of his own which came to be known as Gonville Hall. This in turn was re-founded by the celebrated Dr John Caius in 1557 giving us the present college of Gonville and Caius.

Corpus Christi, founded in 1352, is unusual in that it is the only college which sprang directly from the members of the town. Two Guilds of the day, the Guild of Corpus Christi and the Guild of the Blessed Virgin Mary, merged their identities in the college but there was a certain degree of self-interest in what they were doing. Their college was to ensure an adequate supply of persons who could offer up suitable prayers to God for the souls of each member of the Fraternity as he departed. Each year members of the town are invited by members of the college to join them at a banquet known as the Queenborough Feast. The occasion deliberately marks the association of town and gown within Corpus Christi.

James Stirling's History Faculty building—one of the most controversial modern buildings at Cambridge.

Sir Hugh Casson's Arts Faculty building at Sidgewick Avenue.

I was privileged to be invited to this function one year and can vouch for its magnificence which is made even more impressive by the appearance on the tables of the historically important and very beautiful college plate.

Christopher Marlowe, Shakespeare's famous contemporary, was a student at the college and one can still see his rooms in the old court. He like most under-graduates wrote items for college performances but little is known today of his career as a student.

While the early colleges were developing, the University itself was becoming a better organised and more powerful body. By the end of the fourteenth century it was governed by a Chancellor who was assisted in his deliberations by the House of Regents which consisted of active teachers, and the House of Non-Regents who were resident members of the University not engaged in teaching. But the old strife with the Bishops of Ely continued, for the Church at that time did not easily give up what it regarded as its rightful areas of responsibility. By 1430 the University was again tackling the Pope about the problem. Pope Martin V clearly approved of the case which was laid before him for he decided to recognise the Chancellor's demand for complete ecclesiastical jurisdiction exclusive of any Archbishop or Bishop.

King's College, probably best known to visitors for its famous and beautiful chapel, was the most notable foundation of the fifteenth century. Henry VI intended it to form part of a double foundation with Eton and in doing this there is some evidence that he was repeating the plan of William of Wykeham who had founded Winchester and New College, Oxford. The fifteenth century also saw the founding of Queens' College by Margaret of Anjou, wife of Henry VI, in 1448. Anyone who looks at the college buildings today with their brickwork, stonework, ornamentation, coats of arms, devices and designs becomes aware of the fact that the history of their establishment and creation is much tied up with the history of England itself. The buildings form a perfect living history lesson and Queens' College is probably the best example we can find of this. When Edward IV came to the throne his wife Elizabeth Woodville became patroness and co-foundress of the college, and not unnaturally this has been described as the first outward symbol of the reconciliation of the houses of York and Lancaster. The association of the two Queens in establishing this beautiful college is indicated today by the apostrophe — Queens' and not Queen's.

The fifteenth century brought two other colleges. Robert Wodelark, himself Provost of King's College, founded St Catharine's in 1473, while a Bishop of Ely, in spite of the antagonism which had existed in the past between the Bishops and the University, himself founded Jesus College.

The University Centre from the Mill Pond. The centre was opened to form a focal point of social life among the growing number of graduates and visiting scholars to Cambridge.

John Fisher was an important figure in English and Cambridge history and he appears in greater detail at a later stage in our story. He was Master of Michaelhouse, later a president of Queens' College, Vice Chancellor of the University in 1501 and was elected Chancellor for life in 1504. He was also the confessor to Lady Margaret Beaufort, mother of Henry VII, a position of some considerable influence, and there is no doubt that he was instrumental in persuading her to re-found God's House (which had been first founded in 1439) which then became known as Christ's College. Fisher was the first holder of the Professorship of Divinity which Lady Margaret founded in 1502. This is the oldest professorship in the University and one which still carries her name. Before her death in 1509 Lady Margaret approved the foundation of a new college which was to take the place of the old Hospital of St John. Not surprisingly the college became the present day St John's College and consisted of a Master and thirty-one Fellows. It came into being in 1511.

Here then is our framework. On the surface it may appear as little more than a collection of beautiful buildings but in the succeeding chapters we shall see that there is some entertaining flesh to be put on these elderly but distinguished bones.

The Fitzwilliam Museum.

CHAPTER THREE

Peterhouse and Clare

A PART from being the oldest college at Cambridge, Peterhouse is also one of the smallest, and almost as if it specialises in the slightly unusual it never has the word "college" attached to its name. Peterhouse is always known simply as "Peterhouse" and anyone who refers to it as "Peterhouse College" is likely to earn some very odd looks. As a collection of buildings it has considerable charm and is the first college one comes to when entering Cambridge from the south on the Trumpington Road. Tucked in alongside the massive Fitzwilliam Museum it can easily be overlooked by anyone travelling at modest speed in a car. Its elegant railings carry burnished gold points which glitter in the sun, while across Trumpington Street, divorced from the college itself, is the equally elegant Master's Lodge.

Whenever I think of Peterhouse an image springs to mind which is neither historic nor architectural. It is simply the deep green and bright scarlet and pinks of the magnificent geraniums which the head gardener always achieves for the numerous window boxes and superb hanging baskets with which the buildings are dressed during the summer months. Visitors to Cambridge are always intrigued by the sight of water running down special gulleys on either side of the road outside the college. Hobson, the famous carrier who gave his name to the phrase "Hobson's choice",* is generally given the credit for establishing these runnels in order that livestock driven along the road in the days when animals were moved in such a fashion, might never want for a drink. They also serve as a street cleaning agency since litter and dust which blows into them is carried away by the running water. Although some people today attempt to have them filled in, such ideas are always very strongly opposed.

But Peterhouse is in a position to challenge this for there is no doubt that much of credit should go to Dr Andrew Perne, who although a graduate of St John's became Master of Peterhouse in 1553. As a man he made a great impact upon the college although he was not universally liked and was inclined to blow with the wind in his political and religious views. But both Town and University benefitted when in the year of the Great Plague in 1574 he suggested bringing water from Shelford village, about six miles south of the town, via a special brook in order that it might flow into the filthy King's Ditch and keep it clean, or as Perne put it, "for the perpetual scouring of the same." Unfortunately Perne's water supply became dissipated in several directions once it reached the town and lacked the pressure to scour the King's Ditch, a massive dike which originally formed part of the defences of the town. The Ditch has long since been buried

*Hobson ran a livery stable: he allowed customers no choice of horse to hire, merely allocated them one; thus giving rise to the phrase.

from sight but when Cambridge City Council* closed its Lion Yard car park recently prior to building the new multi-deck park Dr John Alexander of the University of London took the opportunity to organise a quick dig before the contractors' equipment moved in. He uncovered the King's Ditch, probably the last time it will be seen for hundreds of years, and discovered that the black soil and slime with which it was filled in still had a very nasty smell. Henry III encountered the same problem when he made an order for the Ditch to be cleaned out during his reign, and when in 1522 a culvert was constructed at the point where the Ditch passed under Jesus Lane, six cart loads of manure were removed from it. It is not often that archaeologists are able to unearth a genuine medieval smell!

A wander round the buildings of Peterhouse is pleasant but not exhausting, for the entire college grounds are not much more than three hundred feet deep and only a hundred yards or so wide. The magnificent and famous library bequeathed to the college by Dr Perne is on the left as one passes the porter's lodge while the chapel on the immediate right was built by Matthew Wren who was Master from 1626 to 1634. This Wren had a brother who was the father of the famous Sir Christopher Wren and clearly the urge to build ran in the family. Matthew Wren organised the funds for the chapel building and had a strong influence upon its design, but it is only fair to say that the present building has undergone a number of modifications over the years including some at the hands of the Puritans.

Many famous names in English history and literature are connected with Peterhouse. The poet Thomas Gray occupied rooms in the Burrough Building having obtained a scholarship in 1734. It was while at Peterhouse that his famous *Elegy in a Country Churchyard* was written and the manner in which it evokes the peaceful passing of an English day is not altogether foreign to the character of Gray himself. He was not one for rough sports or energetic pastimes and the story of how he came to leave Peterhouse and book himself in at Pembroke College, which is just across the road, is highly amusing. Two or three young men who shared the same staircase intentionally disturbed him with their riots and were frequently known to wake him in the middle of the night. Gray, alarmed by their behaviour, fixed a bar across his window and kept a rope ladder in his rooms. Inevitably he was aroused by shouts in the middle of the night and was promptly scared out of his wits by a fire of wood shavings which had been lit on the staircase by the practical jokers. Gray took to his escape route and descended his rope ladder into St Mary's Churchyard next door and into a barrel of water which the jokers had placed there to cushion his landing. He left for Pembroke where the Master received him "civilly." Not all the details of this story are verifiable but the order for the rope ladder appears among Gray's correspondence and the bar remains on his window to this day.

*Cambridge became a City in 1951.

The oldest part of Peterhouse, itself the earliest Cambridge college. These Hall buildings date from the thirteenth century.

Pembroke has also made its contribution to the sciences. Lord Kelvin, the originator of the Kelvin scale of temperature, was a senior Fellow at the college and his work on the low temperature characteristics of gases was taken up by yet another Peterhouse resident, Sir James Dewar, Jacksonian Professor of Experimental Philosophy and Fullerian Professor at the Royal Institution. Henry Cavendish, who was eventually to give his name to the Cavendish Laboratory at Cambridge, spent four years at Peterhouse, although he never took a degree. He might properly be described as the original mad scientist for he was excessively shy and seldom ever spoke. Under extreme pressure he might speak a word or two to a man but never to a woman. He feared women to a point at which he could not bring himself to look at one and communicated with his female servants by notes. Any girl who crossed his path in his house was immediately discharged. He built a separate entrance so that he could come and go alone and his library was four miles away in order that he could work without the possibility of disturbance. In the end he literally insisted on dying alone. His only love was scientific research which he pursued with great ability for sixty years. At the age of forty he inherited a vast fortune but paid no attention to it and continued living exactly as before. On his death it was virtually untouched. He was the first man to calculate the exact mass of the earth which turned out to be 6,600,000,000,000,000,000,000 tons with a density of about five and a half times that of water. The brilliant Newton, who was at Trinity, had guessed that it might come to something like that a century before!

Whilst at Peterhouse, Cavendish was a Fellow Commoner and failed his

Hanging baskets of flowers are always a feature of the First Court of Peterhouse, during the summer months.

degree examinations miserably because he was too nervous to speak to his professors. He left the college in 1753 and died in 1810, one of the most remarkable figures of his age.

It was the same concern for the effects of the plague which caused Dr Perne to look to the water supply, which resulted in the foundation of the second oldest college at Cambridge. Lady Elizabeth de Clare, widow of John de Burgh, was deeply affected by the impact of the plague on many walks of life. In particular she was concerned about the future supply of clerks, and as patroness of the original foundation of University Hall which had been set up by the University itself in 1326, she felt that the time had come to do something about it. She decided to change the character of University Hall so that it should be the means, not only of keeping teachers in Cambridge but of bringing poor boys of ability to the University. It was as well that she took this sort of interest for there is no doubt that University Hall was a particularly poor body and its endowments were totally inadequate to enable it to become a really effective establishment. There were certain legal impediments to Lady Clare's proposals, for any changes could only be undertaken with the consent of the University. But she was clearly a woman of great determination and in February 1346 journeyed to Cambridge and successfully overcame any possible opposition. After further legal steps the King issued a licence on June 15th for the further endowment of the college and without any sharp break, University Hall became known as Clare Hall.

Even so the problems of lack of money were not finally overcome until 1352 when at Lady Clare's insistence the King sent a commission to investigate. It was an unhappy state of affairs which came to light for financial difficulties had led the Fellows to adopt various dishonest expedients. Robert Spalding, for example, had appropriated and sold a student hostel of which he was tenant-in-chief. Others had obtained benefices which could be had without leaving Cambridge. Lady Clare worked towards the solution of this sort of problem by insisting that as soon as a Fellow's independent income reached ten marks he was to leave the college, a decision which established her as a woman of considerable political ability. Indeed it was Lady Clare who first conceived the idea of a college as a community consisting of undergraduates as well as a Master, Fellows and graduates.

Today, the buildings on the original site are small, compact and among the most charming to be found in Cambridge. In Lady Clare's day the college was on an even more diminutive scale. The scholars used the Church of St John Zachary for worship and it was not until Lady Clare's death in 1360 when the college inherited the furnishings of her private chapel that it decided to build one of its own. In 1521 the college suffered a fairly disastrous fire after which the chapel was rebuilt and the library was also reconstructed. It is easy to assume that the early books belonging to the college were all destroyed by the fire, for they undoubtedly disappeared. Inventories which have come down to us not only confirm that books ceased to be on college premises but have provided evidence that the books strayed off in other directions. It is known, for example, that a manuscript in the Bodleian Library at Oxford is almost certainly the one seen by Leland and Bale in the Clare Library. The exact history of the dispersal of Clare books at that time has yet to be established.

It is not the college buildings of Lady Clare that visitors stream through in their thousands today. During the seventeenth and eighteenth centuries they were slowly demolished to make way for new buildings and now none remain. The rebuilding was begun in 1638 but not completed until 1769. Among the first parts to be built was the present very beautiful bridge over the River Cam. It was built by Thomas Grumbold who was also paid three shillings for a plan of it. The bridge was the first at Cambridge in the classical style and there remains controversy as to its designer. The Royal Commission on Historical Monuments say in their report on Cambridge it is presumed to be designed by Grumbold, but Professor Nikolaus Pevsner states categorically "Grumbold can hardly have designed it himself." Clare bridge contains one piece of fun. Along the top are

Wrought iron gates at Clare College.

A solitary sunbather on the lawns of the Fellows' Garden, Clare College. Visitors are admitted at certain times of the day.

what appear to be fourteen stone balls. Even the august Royal Commission report that there are "thirteen and threequarter" balls along the top but they omit the story which goes with the fact that one ball has a neat quarter cut from the back of it. It is said that some Cambridge undergraduates once had a bet as to how many stone balls there were on top of the bridge. One of the group stole out at night and cut a section from the back of one thereby winning the bet and proving all his companions wrong! There are other versions of this story including the highly unlikely one that one of Cromwell's men damaged it. If he did, he made a remarkably neat job. Miss Enid Porter, that noted authority on Cambridge folk lore and customs, has never succeeded in tracing the origins of the missing piece of stone and neither have I, but the gap is there for all to see.

If one wished to be unkind to this charming college one could accuse it of having stagnated from some time in the seventeenth century to the mid-nineteenth century. It was in 1856 that the name was changed from Clare Hall to Clare College and in the last quarter of the nineteenth century under William Loudon Mollison, who later became Master, there came new life and an gradual increase in undergraduate membership. This process went along so steadily that the traditional buildings and site of the college could no longer hold its members and after the First World War a fund was started to commemorate those who had fallen. Eventually Memorial Court was built on the other side of the river to designs by Sir Giles Gilbert Scott, making Clare College the first Cambridge college to house undergraduates to the west of the river. After the Second World War a further extension was added by the same architect again to provide additional accommodation and remember the fallen. These later buildings are all on the same axis as the University Library and provide a most impressive approach to it.

Many outstanding men have been at Clare but I am certain that one of the most fascinating was Nicholas Ferrar who was born in 1593. He was so bright a child that he entered the college at the age of thirteen while his tutor observed "God keep Nick in a right mind and way; for if he should turn schismatic or heretic he would make work for all the world; such a head, such a heart, such prevalent arguments he hath. . . that I know not who will be able to grapple with him." Ferrar suffered greatly from the Cambridge climate which was fenny and foggy in those days and travelled a great deal for his health. Eventually he settled in London, became Deputy to the Virginia Company* and elected a Member of Parliament in 1624. A year later when the plague struck he and his family moved to Little Gidding in Huntingdonshire where he spent the rest of his life with his family gathered about him and in founding a type of Protestant Retreat. This was described by the Puritans as an "Arminian Nunnery" and was duly broken up about ten years after Ferrar's death.

All Cambridge colleges have interesting collections of plate and silver and Clare is no exception. But in addition to its early treasures it also has three pieces which are of modern interest. There is a silver gilt cup presented by officers of the First Battalion of the King's Shropshire Light Infantry and a statuette representing an officer, a member of the college, of the Prince of Wales Leinster Regiment. This was given by officers of the Second Battalion in recognition of the hospitality these two Battalions received from the college while waiting orders in Cambridge in 1914 to go on active service.

The third piece of this period was presented in June 1919 by ten members of the United States Army who spent the time between the Armistice and their return to America as undergraduates of Clare.

*A Company set up with the object of finding gold and a short route to Cathay.

CHAPTER FOUR

Pembroke and Gonville and Caius

IN 1347 there were only four colleges in Cambridge; Peterhouse and Clare, and Michaelhouse and King's Hall both of which were later to be absorbed into Trinity College. Most of the students within the University lived in lodgings or hostels and it was not long before the advantages of a fully endowed college with its members living on the premises became more and more obvious. This was one of the factors which brought the next batch of colleges into existence over a comparatively short space of time between the years 1347 and 1352. These were to be Pembroke, Gonville Hall, Trinity Hall and Corpus Christi.

Pembroke is a college of great charm which lies just across the Trumpington Road opposite Peterhouse. It lends its name to Pembroke Street which runs along its northern border and provides pedestrians, who are quick enough to realise the possibilities, with a splendid alternative route from Tennis Court Road through to Trumpington Street instead of the more mundane walk along Pembroke Street. It is not one of the famous walks like King's and the Backs but the path crosses New Court with its stately trees and open lawns and then takes a zigzag route under ancient brick archways, through the Hall Screens and Ivy Court and then out under the main archway and into the street. I know the gardeners at Pembroke and they take a professional pride in the appearance of the college. Each season brings its problems and each problem forms the subject for a chat. Anyone who wonders how Cambridge colleges achieve such verdantly green grass should spend ten minutes listening to the professionals describing the treatment their lawns receive each year. They lavish as much care on a patch of grass as many plant specialists devote to their favourite variety. The results are magnificent. "It's greening up well" is a favourite Pembroke phrase when talking of the lawns. One feels that they could not be greener.

Pembroke's Coat of Arms give a splendid clue as to its origins. They contain an "orle of martlets" for Valence and "a label of five points azure" for St Pol. Mary de St Pol, Countess of Pembroke was the second wife of Aymer de Valence when she married him at the age of twenty in 1321. He was a man of great influence with Edward II and is reputed to have led the king away from danger when he lost the battle of Bannockburn. Aymer de Valence fought on behalf of the king in Kent, in Wales and then against the Scots. At last, in the winter of 1323 Aymer appeared to have had a few minutes to himself and was taking things a little easier in his East Anglian domains when he was suddenly despatched as ambassador to France. Inevitably there was trouble brewing, but after some success on the diplomatic front he was returning to England when at Miville on the Seine he got up to take a stroll in his Chamber after dinner and suddenly fell,

Sir Christopher Wren's chapel at Pembroke.

speechless. In a few hours he was dead. Some said it was God's anger at the part he played against the Lancastrians, others claimed it was poison. Apoplexy is now considered to have been the cause although today we would probably speak of it as a stroke. But so sudden and clean a death did not prevent a totally untrue legend springing up at a later date. Through confusion with one of his successors to the Earldom of Pembroke it was said that Aymer died on the morning of his wedding thus leaving Mary St Pol, foundress of the college, "maid, wife and widow all in a day."

Edward III granted her a Charter to found a House of Scholars at Cambridge but before it took on its present title of Pembroke it was sometimes known as the Hall of Valence Marie. Mary de St Pol remains an elusive figure. No picture of her has come down to us and even the portrait in the college hall is based on an eighteenth century fiction. Other representations of her are probably purely conventional and in any case are generally too small to be of any real value in giving us an idea of her appearance. As with many Cambridge colleges the original Statutes of Pembroke are interesting. They contain an ingenious clause setting up a sort of internal espionage system in which students were asked to report their comrades if they drank too much, or if they were quarrelsome, extravagant or visited disreputable shows! One cannot even begin to imagine what would happen if anyone tried to introduce such a system at a University today.

Marie de St Pol also founded Denny Abbey which was not far from the Fenland village of Waterbeach. It was there that she was subsequently buried and even in this she remains elusive. Denny now consists of a farmhouse and when this was bought by the college in 1929 no trace of the foundress's tomb remained.

As with other Cambridge colleges Pembroke has had its share of famous men and in this the evidence is a little more tangible and positive than that of the elusive founder. Probably the best known was William Pitt. His father, Lord Chatham, sent his rather sickly son up to Pembroke at the age of fifteen with an accompanying letter which stated the case quite clearly.

"He is of tender age, and of a health not yet firm enough to be indulged to the full in the strong desire he has to acquire useful knowledge. An ingenious mind and docility of temper will, I know render him comfortable to your discipline, in all points. Too young for the irregularities of a man, I trust, he will not, on the other hand, prove troublesome by the Puerile sallies of a Boy. Such as he is I am happy to place him at Pembroke, and I need not say, how much of his Parents Hearts goes along with him.

I am with great esteem and regard,
Sir
your most faithful and most obedient humble Servant,
CHATHAM

35

The phrase "such as he is" proved prophetic for not long after arriving at the college Pitt was taken seriously ill and his old family nurse Mrs Sparry and Lord Chatham's own doctor hurried to Cambridge to find him being well looked after by Dr Glyn. This is the origin of the erroneous legend, current from the early nineteenth century, that Pitt was so young when he arrived at Pembroke that he was accompanied by his nurse. He proved to be a remarkable student and took his M.A. without any examination because his health had prevented him from keeping to the prescribed terms. Even so he became Chancellor of the Exchequer by the age of twenty-three and Prime Minister at twenty-five. Today a large bronze statue of William Pitt dominates the Chapel Court and this like Pitt himself had a strange history before it came to rest at Pembroke. It was executed by Sir Richard Westmacott and belonged at one stage to the office of the National Debt in Old Jewry, London, appropriately hidden down a side street from the Bank of England. It was Pitt who founded the sinking fund to cope with the National Debt, hence his statue, which was displaced when the present building of the National Debt replaced a bombed out one just after the war. Poor Pitt's statue was sent to an establishment for homeless statues kept by the Ministry of Public Buildings and Works at Hyde Park. Once a year a little money was allowed to pay for a wash and brush up and necessary maintenance.

And there Pitt languished until he was offered to the college and duly accepted in 1969. A large crane hoisted him into position and there he sits today casting a beaky look at the rooms he occupied when of a living and yet less robust constitution.

If Cambridge was never intended for the motor car it was certainly well

Two views of the grounds of Pembroke. The statue is of Sir William Pitt and has found a permanent home in the gardens of his old college.

tailored to the pedestrian. We have seen how Pembroke grounds make a splendid diversion for the person on foot, and the next college to be founded, Gonville and Caius, is also best appreciated on foot. Gonville and Caius lies at the opposite end of King's Parade, a half mile or so from Pembroke. Turn left at the famous Senate House building from which all University affairs are governed by the members of the Regent House who meet there, and walk down Senate House Passage. Half way down on the right the most magnificently ornate doorway presents itself. This is the Gate of Honour of Caius College and is a perpetual reminder of the great love for symbolism possessed by the original Dr Caius. He so arranged the college in his day that the student arriving at the establishment entered through the Gate of Humility. He proceeded via the Gate of Virtue and eventually left through the Gate of Honour. I have no doubt that quite a few would have left through the Gate of Disgrace had there been one, but this was one aspect of academic life which Dr Caius seems to have overlooked.

As with many colleges Gonville and Caius was preceded by an earlier foundation of a different name and was refounded in due course. It began life as Gonville Hall, otherwise known as the Hall of the Annunciation of the Blessed Virgin, which must have proved a considerable mouthful in general conversation. Edmund Gonville was the younger son of William Gonville, a Frenchman domiciled in England. He entered the church and became Rector of Thelnetham in Suffolk in 1320. In 1326 he moved to Rushworth and later, in 1342, to Terrington, both in Norfolk. The fact that Gonville was clearly interested in founding something is suggested by the manner in which he established a college for secular priests at Rushworth in 1342 and after his move to Terrington founded, or at least richly endowed, the Hospital of St John at Lynn. Little is known about his reasons for founding a college at Cambridge, but the fact that Pembroke, Gonville Hall, Trinity Hall and Corpus Christi all came into existence within a decade proves that the idea of this form of foundation was very popular, and indeed fashionable, at the time.

However obscure the reasoning, there are some fairly obvious influences at work if one looks at Gonville's background. For example he was a friend of William Bateman, Bishop of Norwich, who had himself been educated at Cambridge and who may have been planning his own foundation at Trinity Hall. Gonville officially founded Gonville Hall in 1348 two years before his death. He left a considerable sum in the hands of Bishop Bateman who is recorded as the second founder of the college. Between Bateman, who undoubtedly kept the college on its feet during some very difficult times and the arrival of Dr Caius there is a gap of some two hundred years. Caius was to become the third founder after first being appointed as Master of Gonville Hall. Even with Caius the links are not broken for he came from Norwich and was the sixteenth Master of the college when he took up office. In addition he had been a scholar at Gonville Hall

After passing through the Gate of Humility (left), the new student at Gonville and Caius would approach, as in this picture, the Gate of Virtue. Somewhere near this pathway, and before the college was built, Siberch set up his press to print the first book to be produced in Cambridge. The Gate of Honour (right) through which the successful scholar traditionally left the college. It was built in 1575 to Dr Caius' own design.

in 1529 and even at that time showed some of the flair which was later to enable him to become nine times President of the Royal College of Physicians.

His combined offices of Master and Founder are unique in the history of Cambridge colleges and it was not a great success. He was conservative in outlook and is reported to have had a harsh, domineering temper. His many difficulties with the Fellows of the college came to a head in December 1572 when his rooms, in which he had "much Popish trumpery" were pillaged and sacked by his colleagues who were acting at the instigation of the University authorities. He resigned the next year and died a month later in London. His body was returned to Cambridge for burial in the college chapel. Clearly, in spite of the animosities during his lifetime, members of the college were prepared to offer him due recognition in death. There is some evidence that Caius was thinking of some suitable epitaph even during life for at the beginning of July 1573 he ordered a "sepulchrum concameratum." Whether or not this eventually became the magnificent edifice to Caius which now stands within the college chapel we shall probably never know, but for all his faults Caius' name was perpetuated in breathtaking style. His monument was carved by "Theodore and others" and consists of a wall monument with tomb chest and canopy. It is richly decorated with much strapwork and decorative panels. At the centre is the achievement of arms of Caius linked by bands enscribed "Fui Caius" with recesses containing carved fruits and flowers with spandrels bearing the sangrene (houseleek) and flower gentle (maranth) for immortality.

In company with many other colleges of the present day Caius is not blessed with much space into which it can expand. When in 1885 it was decided to lay out a new Fellows' garden it had to be done at Newham and not many years later the college acquired houses on the south side of that quaint little pedestrian way, Rose Crescent. In 1901 these were demolished and rebuilt as St Michael's Court while as recently as 1934 a large block of buildings incorporating commercial shops and premises were built nearby on the north side of Cambridge Market Hill. This today is that rather impressive block which faces the tourist when he stands on the steps of the Guildhall and looks across the square at the spot where Hobson's Conduit,* or fountain head, used to stand.

*Moved in 1855 to the corner of Lensfield Road and Trumpington Road where it stands to-day.

The door in the wall. When the sixteenth century library was built at Trinity Hall a walkway led to the Master's Lodge. Today only the door remains.

CHAPTER FIVE

Trinity Hall and Corpus Christi

TRINITY Hall and Corpus Christi complete the sudden spate of college founding which characterised Cambridge between 1347 and 1352. Both sets of buildings today give us an excellent idea of what the medieval college possessed in its essential character. In the case of Corpus Christi the oldest court is very little altered from its original state and is undoubtedly the best preserved example of a medieval college court in Cambridge. If one synthesised the building plans of the earliest parts of Pembroke, Gonville, Trinity Hall and Corpus an interesting picture would emerge of the true college layout of this period. From the ground plan we can learn something of the climate and general conditions under which members of a collegiate community had to live. For example the living rooms were usually placed on the south side because this was the warmer aspect of the college and with primitive heating, warmth could be important during the exceptionally cold winters of that period.

It would have been reasonable to assume that the architects of the day, when faced with the task of housing a group of people in building blocks would have adopted the technique of the inns, in which the various rooms were connected by means of outside balconies or galleries reached by a single staircase. Instead, castle building seems to have provided the influence in which, in the towers at least, a number of doors were arranged to open onto a single staircase. The main court of the college was entered through its main gateway and immediately opposite was generally the hall and buttery separated by a central passage. About ten such courts survive in very much their original form in Cambridge. The halls were mostly heated by a brazier with a central roof opening to carry away the fumes. The Master of the college, a single man because celibacy was still the rule, lived in two rooms and it is noticeable that these were often positioned in such a way that he could observe what went on in the hall and the chapel without being overlooked himself!

Trinity Hall, in many ways typical of the period, seemed to find an admirable way of advertising itself to the visitor approaching the town, so good in fact that today's visitor can still get his first sight of the college sixteen miles from Cambridge if he has sharp eyes. In 1597 an estate at Walpole St Peter was bought by the college from a bequest by William Mowse and a further handsome gift from Robert Hare. The income was held in trust until quite recently for repairing the roads around Cambridge, particularly the road to Barkway. Trinity Hall marked the route with a special set of milestones which remain at the roadside today. On the first and sixteenth milestones respectively are the coats of arms of

Mowse and Hare. All the others carry the Arms of Trinity Hall; "Sable a crescent within a border ermine." The stones were erected sometime between 1725 and 1732 and they remain in a remarkable state of preservation.

As old as the milestones is the basic purpose of Trinity Hall which was to provide men well versed in Canon and Civil Law. As a result a long line of Chief Justices have come from this college while between 1512 and 1803 the four hundred doctors of the College of Advocates included nearly two hundred Cambridge men of which nearly eighty were from Trinity Hall. Like Clare College, its immediate neighbour, Trinity Hall is a little difficult for the stranger to find. From Trinity Street it is necessary to dive down Trinity Lane following round the sharp bend to the left. On the right is Trinity Hall, ahead the towers of King's Chapel, whilst just out of sight down the lane is the front of Clare. Gonville and Caius and Trinity Hall have more in common than the closeness of their buildings and their original foundation. William Bateman, who played such a large part in the history of Gonville was the direct founder of Trinity Hall. He was negotiator for Edward III in some difficult international situations and died at Avignon in 1355 while abroad on Edward's behalf. It was probably the shortage of clergy following the plague from May to September 1349 which confirmed and strengthened Bateman's intention to form a college dedicated to the adequate staffing of the nation's churches and courts.

The grounds of Trinity Hall are not large but they do have the advantage, denied to many Cambridge colleges, of backing down to the river. Just before one reaches the river wall stands a charming raised terrace. For most of the year it simply provides a splendid vantage point from which to view the numerous comings and goings of boats and punts along the Cam. From time to time, however, it is transformed into an open air stage from which various college drama groups present everything from Shakespeare to Ibsen. Watching Shakespeare in the garden on a warm summer's night with the sun creating a magnificent sky directly behind the players is an experience which is not to be missed. Only the occasional merry cries of a boating party on their way home and the armies of midges who use the river as their base, turn one's attention away from the immortal prose which could have been written for just such a setting. I would suggest that anyone who visits Trinity Hall garden — during daylight that is — should take a close look at the exterior of the fine old library building which juts out into the lawns. On the south side can be seen the curious remains of an old doorway which has long since been bricked up. The fact that it is more than half way up the wall confounds a number of people, but there is a simple explanation. A print by David Loggan in his famous *Cantabrigia Illustrata* shows a wall joining the library to the Master's Lodge which also provided the Master with a closed walk to the library. Eventually the wall was removed, leaving the Master with a slightly more circuitous route to the books.

The interior of the Elizabethan library building is particularly fine. All the heavier books were once attached to their cases by chains and the mountings are still visible. These consist of wrought iron lock plates for the hasps which were in turn hinged to the rods which held the chains. The plates are decorated with the crescent from the arms of the college. Apart from the nearness of their foundation dates, Trinity Hall and Corpus Christi both share excellence in the content, layout and appearance of their libraries. There was a time when colleges did not worry much about the security of their books and plate, because it was argued that each volume and each piece was so valuable and so well known to the antique trade that anyone trying to sell such property would be apprehended immediately. Unfortunately this is no longer the case and a new type of thief has appeared who is highly educated, who knows the content and value of college libraries and who is sufficiently well connected to find private purchasers for his gains, even though they are known to be stolen. More and more the colleges of Cambridge are coming to seek expert advice in the installation of sophisticated burglar alarm systems. Corpus Christi has taken many steps to protect its books and its plate and well it might, for it has one of the finest collections of plate in Cambridge in addition to its rare and valuable books. To quote them all would take a volume in itself, but I think we can pause and consider two items. Of the books, one of the most interesting is an example of a volume printed by Johann or John Siberch, the first man to ever print books in Cambridge. It is called *De Conscribendis Epistolis,* was

Visitors walk through Trinity Hall.

written by Erasmus and was published in 1521. Siberch set up his press in a house which was later removed to make way for Gonville and Caius College. Twenty pounds was borrowed from the University Chest to help establish him in business but he did not stay long. He returned to Germany and his marital troubles and never paid back the money. An amusing sidelight to this occurred in July 1971 when as part of the celebrations of the printing of the first book in Cambridge, Mr Brooke Crutchley, the Cambridge University Printer, paid back the money on Siberch's behalf. Fortunately the University authorities waived their rights to any interest on the loan. Had they insisted it would have amounted to £68,582,699,000 based on a modest return of five per cent!

The other item at Corpus Christi which must now be of considerable value is a small wooden bowl or mazer, edged in gold, which is reputed to be the oldest piece of college plate in Cambridge. When I attended the famous Queenborough Feast at Corpus Christi this famous mazer was on the table in front of me.

The Queenborough Feast commemorates the rather unusual origins of Corpus Christi. It is the only college to have been directly founded by representatives of the Town of Cambridge and Lord Queenborough left it money to finance an annual feast to which representatives of the town are invited by members of the college. Thus all round the hall, town and university members alternate in a manner which helps one to forget the emnity which once existed between them. As in most towns at the time Cambridge had its share of Guilds and it was two of these, the Guild of Corpus Christi and the Guild of the Virgin Mary which joined forces to found the present college. The Guild of Corpus Christi had its headquarters just to the south of the churchyard of St Benet's and when they had established their college they incorporated the church by building a gallery between the two. I fancy that the two Guilds were not purely concerned with "training persons up in academical learning" for they also insisted that there should be members of the college available to offer a quick prayer to God every time the soul of a member of the Fraternity departed this life. Bearing in mind the impetus of the Black Death one can see the reasoning behind this clever piece of self-interest. For years Corpus Christi had the working title of "Benet College" and it was not until 1827 when the old entrance by the churchyard was closed and the new court opening into Trumpington Street was built, that the name was lost.

Probably the best known member of the college throughout its long history was Christopher Marlowe, although it was rich in many other poets and literary men. Marlowe had a room in Old Court which is now marked for visitors by a special stone let into the wall, but this has not always been the case. The Rev. H. P. Stokes in his history of the college observed "It has pleased the college authorities studiously to ignore the existence of this celebrated man. Masters in his history of the college has not mentioned his name and Dr Lamb is equally

Corpus Christi. The main gate.

silent. Even in the List of Members the name 'Marlin' is simply recorded without a footnote." Thomas Legge and John Fletcher were also Corpus men. They are not quite so well known as Marlowe but in their day their work was considered of equal standing.

Anyone interested in the history of sport must also take note of Corpus Christi. Willis and Clarke in their famous *Architectural History of the University of Cambridge* say that the earliest recorded reference to the game of tennis was at the college. Here it was recorded that the walls of a building which had been intended for a bakehouse and granary were carried up to their full height between 1487 and 1515. They were definitely used as a court in which to play 'hand tennis'. In 1569 they were turned into rooms for students and a second tennis court was probably built soon afterwards. It is shown in Hammond's map of Cambridge dated 1592 and in Loggan's view of the college drawn in or about 1688. This second tennis court had a roof and was in use for nearly two hundred years before being pulled down in 1756. The college was also well known for its bowling green and this is also illustrated by both Loggan and Hammond. Corpus Christi as the home of English tennis is still marked to this day, for the road which runs nearby is named 'Tennis Court Road.'

Corpus Christi, Old Court, one of the best preserved medieval college courts at Cambridge. Christopher Marlowe, the contemporary of Shakespeare, had rooms in this court.

CHAPTER SIX

King's and Queens'

A GAP of about fifty years divides King's College and Queens' College from the brisk appearance of their predecessors. Considered against the total age of Cambridge and its university and college buildings, this is not much, but in reality the distance is large. To anyone who looks at King's College — in fact there are over eighty thousand visitors a year — it is obvious that the general scale and conception of the place is vastly different from the medievalism of the charmingly compact Corpus Christi. Queens', on the other hand, represents an even bigger jump into the future. The President's half timbered building was the first and the only college building so constructed to reach down to the present day. In one spectacular leap we have arrived in Tudor England. King's College is of totally difference character architecturally, but it too demonstrated a breadth of vision and a stylish way of doing things which previous colleges were either too poor or humble to contemplate.

King's and Queens' have one other difference which the reader might like to note. Neither college has a Master. Instead the head of the establishment is called a Provost in the case of King's and the President at Queens'. King's College with its famous Chapel and its spacious open lawns has become very much the trademark of Cambridge. The facade, which is relatively modern, occupies one side of King's Parade, surely one of the most impressive and charming stretches of street anywhere in the world. Such vistas have, for so long, provided Cambridge as a city and town with considerable and complicated planning problems when trying to meet the constantly changing pattern of life. King's Chapel and King's Parade represents such a standard of excellence in town planning that it is almost embarrassing for modern man to attempt anything for himself in their shadow. And yet there is a curious affinity between the Cambridge of today and the problems under which it labours, and the days of Henry VI when he first decided that he would found a college at Cambridge. Twentieth century Cambridge residents are quite used to the appearance of the statutory notices and the bulldozer as another part of the city is requisitioned for new building and promptly knocked down. It was the same in Henry's day, for before he could start work on his college he had to carry out a very similar operation, buying up large parts of the busy riverside complex of quays and warehouses which stood on the land he wished to use. As Henry's commissioners visited the tiny bustling streets and marked out the pieces they wanted I have no doubt the reaction of the citizens was not unlike that of today!

Henry VI was nineteen years old when he conceived the original idea for his college, but of his boldly declared plan only the famous chapel was completed according to his wishes. I always feel that history has been most unkind to Henry. The allegations that he spent a period of madness have never seemed to make sense in the light of modern medical knowledge and thinking. I think it is clear that he was an incredibly sensitive and religious person who never considered himself ideally suited for the rigorous, even belligerent, duties of Kingship. Anyone who studies the pressures under which he worked must come to the conclusion that his 'madness' was no more than a form of mental breakdown. In pre-Freudian days, however, such a concept just did not exist. King's Chapel itself is such a magnificent building that even if Henry did have a period of genuine insanity there is no doubt in my mind that he was also blessed with periods of the most divine lucidity. Such a concept at the age of twenty-one does rather tend to take one's breath away.

His aim in founding a college at Cambridge was to "Extirpate heresies, to increase the number of clergy and to provide ministers of religion whose life and doctrine would give light to his subjects." Henry also founded Eton and to this day a strong link, or "treaty of perpetual friendship" as it was called, has existed between the two. Originally the college at Cambridge was to be called "St Nicholas" on whose day, December 6th, Henry was born. He laid the first stone of his new college on April 2nd 1441, but by 1443 growth had been rapid and the members were petitioning for a larger establishment altogether. By letters patent of the same year the college was re-named the "King's College of St Mary and St Nicholas at Cambridge" and its size increased. Scholars from Eton were to be transferred to it "when sufficiently imbued with the rudiments of grammar."

Today the principal glory is undoubtedly the chapel and the college grounds are always thronged with visitors. Rubens' "Adoration of the Magi" now forms the altarpiece for the chapel, having been placed there as part of the recent cleaning and restoration scheme undertaken by the college, and carried out under the direction and to the design of Sir Martyn Beckett.* The glass windows are magnificent and among the finest examples of their type in Europe. Such is the overwhelming impact of the place with its superb fan vaulted roof and intricate organ screen that it tends to obscure the mass of tiny yet interesting detail to be found all over it. I would mention the initials of Henry VIII who helped complete the building and Anne Boleyn cut in the screen. Most people walk right by them and yet they drive home the essentially personal nature of the interest of various monarchs in the college and its buildings.

It is tempting to talk at length about the architecture of King's. Instead I will refer the reader to the Gibbs building which nearly abuts the chapel and the new range of buildings which form part of a post-war joint scheme carried out by King's and its neighbouring college, St Catharine's. It is now extremely difficult to

*This is fully described in *King's College Chapel, Cambridge*, by Rodney Tibbs. Terence Dalton Limited, 1970.

King's College Chapel and the Gibbs building.

make out where one college finishes and the other begins. Vast movable sets of iron railings allow the two buildings to flow into each other on special occasions and with these pulled back a rather charming court of the traditional style is revealed.

King's has never been blessed with the battery of household historical names of which many Cambridge colleges can boast. Probably the best known in recent years was the poet, Rupert Brooke. His was very much a family connection, for a generation earlier, after successive waves of reform had loosened the grip of Eton and its pupils on the college, W. P. Brooke, Rupert's father, became the first non-Etonian to be elected into a Fellowship. The college has an early link with the literary world as well, for Thomas Thomas, a Fellow of the college, was the first official university printer to hold the office, or at least the first holder actually to print books. It was Henry VIII who granted to Cambridge University the right to "three stationers, or printers or sellers of books." The date was 1534 and from that day to this the University has maintained that it made them

The Victorian post box outside King's.

Queens' College, the River Cam and the Mathematical Bridge which was built in 1749 without nails and relying purely on pegs to hold it together. It was rebuilt in 1867 and again in 1902.

independent of London printers and the exclusive licences they previously held. Although they had no specific licence to print the Bible, such as that granted to the Queen's printers, they have always stood by their right to do so; indeed Cambridge University Press has long printed bibles, including the latest revised version.

It was the arrival of printing and the subsequent ability to print the classics which had one of the most profound effects upon the University and its teaching at that time. Strong humanist ideas were beginning to make themselves felt, influenced to a large extent by the arrival in Cambridge of such men as Erasmus, the great Dutch scholar, who was patronised by Bishop Fisher. Fisher had the ear of the Lady Margaret Beaufort, mother of Henry VII, and was able to direct much of her attention and wealth to Cambridge.

Erasmus was lodged at Queens' College in 1506 and although his period in Cambridge was not a particularly happy one for himself, there is no doubt that he and one or two others did much to bring about the swing away from the old ruts into which teaching had fallen, and to lead it towards the "new learning." In 1513 Cambridge suffered from the plague and letters written by Erasmus show that he was not particularly happy with the presence of the disease or his insularity from the continent. He complained that his expenses were high and his profits small. However, he held Lady Margaret's divinity professorship and his presence helped to raise the prestige of Cambridge at this time.

Originally Queens' College was known as the College of St Bernard, and although Henry VI granted a new charter in 1448 he was soon being petitioned by Margaret of Anjou, his wife, to refound the college, no doubt at the instigation of Andrew Doket, Rector of St Botolphs, who had originally obtained a charter himself in 1446. There is an interesting point for the Women's Liberation Movement here which I have not yet heard them quote. Margaret wanted a college at Cambridge "to laud and honneure of sexe feminine" since there was no college in the university founded by a Queen of England. Again the Foundation procedure was invoked and the present college of Queens' received its charter in 1448. But the college did not get its Statutes at that time and as far as is known none were framed during the reign of Henry VI. It was not until Edward IV became monarch that we find Elizabeth his wife granted the Statutes and herself becoming Patron of the college. In this way the foundation for the modern spelling of Queens' with the apostrophe after the 's' was being laid. In fact it became the tradition that successive Queens of England were to become patrons of the college. The tradition lapsed in the sixteenth century but was revived in 1948 by Queen Elizabeth, now the Queen Mother.

Fisher, of course, became one of the first Presidents of Queens', an office to which he was appointed while still Chancellor of the University. He held the position while he was engaged in the foundation of one of Margaret Beaufort's colleges, Christ's. He resigned in 1508 on the grounds that his other duties prevented his regular residence at Queens' College. There is no doubt he must have been a very busy man!

Erasmus is remembered today by the Erasmus building. This was built overlooking the river in 1960 and was designed by Sir Basil Spence. Today it is a fairly innocuous building which is beginning to fit happily into its setting, but at the time of its construction it provoked intensive letterwriting to *The Times*. The Backs, it was said would be ruined, but the building, like its namesake, was merely a little ahead of its time.

Throughout the years Queens' has had a fluctuating career. The numbers moved up and down in an alarming manner, largely as the result of the varying stands it took in times of religious change. It supported the Reformation and managed to get the ear of Henry VIII through Thomas Smith who was elected to a Fellowship in 1530. It was Smith who managed to persuade Henry not to deal out the same treatment to the Cambridge colleges as he had the monasteries. He was in a good position to achieve this for he was Principal Secretary of State to Elizabeth I and Edward VI and had clearly developed his statesmanship to a high degree. During the Civil War, the college stood resolutely behind the King. But retribution was not far away and on August 30th 1642 one Captain Oliver Cromwell arrived to arrest Dr Edward Martin, the President of the college at the time. In August of the following year the unfortunate Dr Martin was actually placed under hatches on a ship at Wapping with about eighty other people it was proposed to transport to slavery. Eventually he was restored from exile and reinstated as President in 1660. A number of Royalist Fellows were duly elected but in due course Roundhead Fellows were elected as well. Martin did much to promote subsequent harmony between the two in spite of the manner in which he had suffered during the years of conflict.

Queens' College, First Court. The magnificent sundial is said to have been constructed by Sir Isaac Newton.

The President's Lodge, Queens'. Cambridge's best example of timber-framed building. It dates from the sixteenth century.

CHAPTER SEVEN

St. Catharine's and Jesus

BY THE time Robert Woodlark, or Wodelarke as he is sometimes called, came to found St Catharine's College on St Catharine's Day 1473, he was faced with a modern problem. At least ten collegiate communities occupied the triangle of land bounded by what is now known as The Backs, Trinity Street, King's Parade and Silver Street, and space for development had become the major difficulty. The site he chose was convenient to say the least, for it was next door to King's College, but it was also covered by a conglomeration of inns, houses, tenements, alleyways and streets, one of which was the famous Milne Street, which used to lead down to the riverside. Woodlark began in a modest way acquiring property as he went along. It was to be a tiny college. The entire length of the east side of the original foundation only stretched for 54 to 55 feet and the main entrance was in Milne Street, or as it now is, Queens' Lane.

St Catharine's has always suffered a shortage of space and right up to the present day it has been acquiring suitable property whenever the opportunity arose in order to provide a little more room. Over the years it has acquired the Bull Hotel which stood in Trumpington Street, while the present library stands on the site of the famous stables used by the carrier Hobson. The most recent development at St Catharine's has an almost poetic element of destiny about it, for in conjunction with King's College, its illustrious neighbour, the two colleges have built five new courts which share the land between them. It was partly sheer necessity which brought about such co-operation, but even so it is welcome for it is the first example of such a joint effort between colleges at Cambridge. By tackling the area in such a way it has proved possible to make much better use of the space available than would have been the case with an individual effort. St Catharine's is now one of the very few Cambridge colleges to enjoy the luxury of an underground car park for its members and staff, for the planners insisted that such a park should be built when the new development went ahead. The new rooms also incorporate private baths, a further untold luxury which will be welcomed by the many visitors who arrive to attend such things as the occasional symposium or summer school, with which St Catharine's, like so many Cambridge foundations, attempt to augment their income. At least one authority reports, "Stout Welsh miners have been known to blanch before the communal sanitary appliances of most colleges which are a great deal inferior to pithead baths." Similarly I can recall the Mayor of a northern town who came to Cambridge to attend a conference and was shattered to find extremely antiquated lavatory

55

arrangements in the college rooms (not St Catharine's!) which he was given. He made a great fuss and achieved national publicity. He also changed his mind about the young gentlemen leading a soft life while they were "up."

St Catharine's therefore, both begins and comes up to date with a close relationship with the neighbouring college of King's. Today, the main entrance has been swivelled round and is found on Trumpington Street opposite the main gate of Corpus Christi. It was always known as St Catharine's Hall until comparatively recent times and the Coat of Arms contains a large Catharine Wheel. Probably the most popular connotation of the Catharine Wheel is to be found in fireworks but it originates as the wheel on which St Catharine herself was originally tortured. There has not always been agreement on the exact form of the catharine wheel emblem at the college, for as recently as 1934 York Herald informed the Bursar that the correct Arms were "Gules, a Catharine wheel, Or". There are eight spokes on the wheel with eight knives as continuations of the spokes, but in the records of the college the number of spokes and knives vary. However, York Herald's opinion does agree with the Arms as given in John Ivory's "Foundation of the University of Cambridge", 1672, and with the stone carving which the visitor may see to this day over the archway in Queens' Lane.

In the history of St Catharine's College one or two names are important. One must mention Mrs Mary Ramsden, who by leaving a very large sum of money to the college in 1743, raised it from the level of a rather poor and small institution into something which at least had much brighter possibilities. She founded six fellowships, ten scholarships and erected twelve new sets of rooms to house the the newcomers. Her rather difficult rules helped divide rather than unify the college although her money undoubtedly kept it going as a separate entity during difficult times. The college was again divided and completely ostracised when an election for the Mastership was held in 1861. This has been described as "the greatest disaster in the history of the college". Two candidates were involved and

The catharine wheel is a prominent feature of the Trumpington Street entrance to St Catharine's College.

St Catharine's College.

there were five voters. Charles Robinson secured the Mastership by following an age-old tradition of voting for himself, but the whole business was surrounded by mystery and Francis Jameson, his rival, complained bitterly in various quarters afterwards. Robinson was virtually 'sent to Coventry' by the University which had no right to take sides in the dispute anyway. It took many years for the college to become completely free of the resulting odium.

John Addenbrooke occurs three times in college records for there were three different men of this name. It was the second Addenbrooke who founded the hospital at Cambridge, the old building of which stands not far along Trumpington Street from the college. Prior to 1860 he was the only Fellow to take a medical course at Cambridge and when he died he left his books and his medicine cabinet to the college.

One other name crops up in St Catharine records at frequent intervals. He was a college retainer and he gave rise to the delightful entry in the seventeenth century accounts, "To Batty for mending the bog house, £0 3s. 7d."

By contrast, Jesus College has what the estate agents would call 'a very desirable position.' It is quite close to the shopping centre of Cambridge, yet very secluded, with its main entrance set well back down a brick walled alleyway known throughout the years as The Chimney. This aspect of Jesus did not escape King James the First who is said to have remarked "that if I lived in the University I would pray at King's, eat at Trinity, and study and sleep at Jesus." The college is on the site of a former Benedictine nunnery about which I would dearly like to know more. It was inhabited by "dissolute nuns" and the nunnery, dedicated to St Rhadegund, soon became notorious for extravagance. Bishop Alcock, the founder of Jesus College, visited them in an attempt at moral reformation but it would seem that his efforts met with little success. Eventually only two nuns remained and the Bishop called upon their dilapidated premises again. What he saw is given in the letters patent for the foundation of his college dated June 12 1469. Their "improvidence, extravagence and incontinence" apparently resulted from their proximity to the university. "Only two nuns remain. One is elsewhere, and the other is of ill fame (infamis). They are in abject want, unable to keep up divine services or the works of mercy and piety required of them, and are ready to depart leaving the house desolate."

John Alcock, then Bishop of Ely, called his college "The college of the most Blessed Virgin Mary, St John the Evangelist, and the Glorious Virgin St Rhadegund" who until then had apparently been celebrated by anything but virginity. In spite of a title of such paralysing length it was clear that Alcock wanted his college known as Jesus from the outset and this it has always been. At various points on the college buildings, and in particular over the main gatehouse, Alcock's rebus or emblem appears — a cock sitting on a globe. In a library window one of these birds proclaims, "I am a cock" while another opposite answers, "and I am another."

Much of the nuns' establishment was incorporated into the buildings of Jesus. The nuns' refectory was transformed into the college hall, while their Church was considerably reworked to become a very splendid college chapel. Parts of the earlier buildings can still be seen let into the wall and protected by a railing in Cloister Court. However dissolute the nuns may have been they clearly selected the site with some care and great deal of local knowledge. This was proved as recently as 1947 when the winter, one of the most severe in living memory, was followed by a thaw and very heavy rains. Many Cambridge colleges were flooded, especially those near the river like Queens'. The Cam flooded across Jesus Green up to the boundary of College Close, the land at the rear of Jesus. But the college, on higher and slightly firmer ground, escaped, as it must have done over successive centuries. Not all the buildings at Jesus are ancient. In company with many Cambridge colleges they have been adding buildings to cope with increased numbers, although this college has the advantage of ample space

Coleridge the poet occupied rooms here in Outer Court, **Jesus College**, when **he** was at Cambridge. They were on the ground floor to the right of the archway.

on which to set its plans. The new North Court was designed by David Roberts and built by Rattee and Kett, the local firm which recently restored King's College Chapel. Study bedrooms have been provided for seventy undergraduates with three "sets" each of two rooms for graduates, two three-roomed sets for Fellows, a sick bay and changing rooms for the nearby playing fields.

All this compares lavishly with conditions which existed in 1662, details of which have come down to us through various letters and memoirs. John Strype, a scholar of 1662, assured his mother that food was "good and sufficient". There was roast meat at dinner and supper every day except on Fridays and Saturdays which still remained as fast days. A second course was served four nights a week at high table but not to the undergraduates. Strype did however go to the Buttery for extra bread and beer for breakfast. He also liked hot milk for his breakfast but he had to go outside the college to get it. His room, one of the best in the college and overlooking the Master's garden, cost him ten shillings a year.

Jesus can boast some very famous men. Samuel Taylor Coleridge the poet occupied rooms just to the right of the staircase which is exactly opposite the main gate tower entrance. He arrived at the college on February 5th 1791 and was

Then and now. The Waterhouse building (right) at Jesus College was erected in 1870. Today it is accompanied by a design by David Roberts built in 1966.

On the fifteenth century archway at Jesus is the insignia of the Founder, Bishop Alcock. It is a cock, inscribed *Prosperum iter facias*.

converted to Unitarianism by William Frend, whose feud with the Masters and Fellows over religion itself makes a fascinating chapter of college history. Coleridge was far more than a poet and it was at Jesus that his tremendously wide intellect and range of interests first began to stretch itself. He devoured all types of books and wrote some poetry, items of which appeared in the *Cambridge Intelligencer. A Wish Written in Jesus Wood* belongs to this period as does the very celebrated *Monologue to a Young Jackass on Jesus Piece.*

An earlier and equally famous member of the college was Archbishop Cranmer, who entered Jesus about seven years after it had been opened. There is an amusing sidelight on the state of celibacy in Cranmer's career, for celibacy was insisted on at all Cambridge colleges, especially among Fellows. In about 1511 Cranmer was not only elected to a Fellowship at Jesus but "it chanced him to marry a wife" as his secretary rather oddly put it. She was the daughter of a gentleman and of the wife of the innkeeper of *The Dolphin* which stood at the Bridge Street corner of All Saints Passage. Cranmer vacated his Fellowship on marriage and kept himself solvent by lecturing in theology at the small Benedictine House of Buckingham College, which was later incorporated into Magdalene College. Within a year Cranmer's wife died giving birth to their child. Immediately the Master and Fellows of the college again made him a Fellow of the college, a vote of confidence if ever there was one.

Laurence Sterne, author of *Tristram Shandy* was also at the college, as was Steve Fairbairn the famous oarsman and Sir Arthur Quiller-Couch, 'Q' of literary fame. The notorious William Dowsing was among those who visited the college and a number of chapel fittings were swept away by him. The organ, however, was dismantled and hidden in the Master's orchard! During these troublesome times the college lent support to the King and in 1642 subscribed pieces of plate weighing 1,201 ounces to him to assist the royal cause. There followed such adventures as the arrest of Dr Sterne and a former Master, Dr Beale, while the Fellows voted themselves a prolonged leave of absence! The story of the organ re-appears again when, from college accounts, we learn that in 1746 the college decided to discontinue the salary paid to the organist. The organ, the same one which had been hauled off to the orchard, fell into disrepair although William Cole, the famous historian, has a note about it in his manuscripts. "I was told, Mar. 4 1776, by a Domestick of the College that tho' they have a very good organ in the chapel, to which the singing men used to resort on Surplice Nights, and always made use of in my Time of being in the University, that it is now laid aside as a useless Piece of Lumber and Expence. I suppose the Revenue appropriated to it is now applied to other more profitable uses."

The last stage in the history of the organ must also end our chapter on Jesus. In 1790 the college agreed "to make a present of the remains of our Organ to the Parish of All Saints in Cambridge." Now even All Saints Church is gone.

The Master's Lodge, Jesus College. Considerable alterations were made to this building 1886 when the porch and two-storey bay window were added.

CHAPTER EIGHT

Christ's and John's

TOWARDS the end of the fifteenth century definite changes were beginning to occur in the world of study and scholarship. Apart from the trend towards humanism and more literary studies, which we noted with the emergence of Siberch's press on the site of Gonville and Caius, there was ample evidence that outside Oxford and Cambridge the various grammar schools and other places of study were beginning to gain impetus. Directly connected with this was the foundation by William Byngham of God's House, a college which was to be devoted entirely to the training of schoolmasters. Byngham was a London parish priest and first set up his educational ideal in Milne Street, which as the reader will recall from the chapter on King's College, was very soon commandeered by Henry VI for his rather more magnificent effort.

God's House simply had to be moved, and in due course Byngham took himself and his little foundation off to a spot near Barnwell Gate and just outside the King's Ditch which formed part of the town's fortifications. God's House not only took in grammar schoolmasters, it laid down some strict rules as to what they were to do when it had finished with them. After graduating in grammar they were to accept any post with suitable stipend offered at any school built within the previous forty years. Special lectures were arranged for the autumn term, now part of the long vacation, in order that country schoolmasters might have refresher courses while their schools were closed to allow their pupils to go off and help with the harvest.

Byngham himself took over the Proctorship of his college, as the Head or Master was known, but it was not to be for long. Lady Margaret Beaufort, who features so much in the foundation of Cambridge colleges, was clearly in a mood to launch something new. She had buried her third husband and seen her son, Henry VII, on the throne and no doubt had the time to devote herself to something of the sort. Fisher is usually credited with having turned her mind towards education and it must be admitted that as her confessor he certainly had the opportunity,and as Vice Chancellor of the University he must have had the inclination. Just how she moved in on poor Byngham and spread him the news that he was involved in a take-over is not well recorded, and neither is his reaction to the situation.

Lady Margaret greatly increased the little college in size and up-dated its name from God's House to Christ's College, which is as it stands today. It still occupies the site to which it moved from Milne Street although the whole aspect of the college and its grounds are very much larger as the result of Lady Margaret's work. Anyone who looks into the history of the college is struck by the number of amusing anecdotes which seem to occur. I particularly like the story of the courtier who urged Edward VI to take away some of the Fellowships of the college because it considered itself to be founded on imitation of Christ and the twelve apostles. The king replied that he had a better way of reducing their conceit and promptly added a thirteenth. The money for the additional fellow and three pupil scholars came from the Manor and Parsonage of Bourn which the King gave to the college as some recompense for the continued absence of income from Bromehill Priory.* The first 50 years after Lady Margaret's intervention were continually marked by disputes over the Priory. Henry Lockwood, the master, kept in touch with Thomas Cromwell who had now taken over Wolsey's influence at court in an effort to press the college's point of view. Heavy charges are recorded for travelling up to see Cromwell and it is also clear that on one occasion Cromwell was presented with half a tun of wine. Methods of doing business have not changed much over the years.

Christ's College has always had its share of interesting and gifted men. Richard Clerke, one of the translators of the Bible, was there in the later sixteenth century and so was William Perkins, who distinguished himself by the manner in which he came to give up drink. It seems that he once heard a woman say to a naughty child, "Hold your tongue, or I will give you to the drunken Perkins yonder." It was enough. He never touched a drop after that and became a student in Divinity and lecturer at Great St Andrew's Church which is just across the road from the college. Swans, mulberry trees and the poet Milton are probably the best known elements of the college's past. The college has its own swan mark and has from its earliest days held a royal licence to keep swans. It was in 1608 that it bought three hundred mulberry trees in an effort to please James I who was anxious to start the production of silk in England. These trees were planted during the year of Milton's birth and the tree in the Fellows' garden which is traditionally associated with him may well have been one of these. There is another in the Master's garden. It would be nice to substantiate the popular picture of the youthful Milton rushing round with his spade busily planting them, but like so many of these stories it is impossible to confirm.

Visitors to Cambridge never have to travel far to find Christ's College. It is in the middle of the main shopping area and just off the end of the quaintly named Petty Cury and on the junction of Hobson's Street. It was about the same time as the mulberry trees were being planted and James was expanding the silk industry that Christ's College got itself a water supply from the Gog Magog Hills which lie to the south east of the City. A brook ran from this hill to the southern end of Trumpington Street — indeed it is there to this day — and this was tapped

*Manor of Roydon (Essex) was given to Christ's College by Lady Margaret as part of its original endowment. It was surrendered to Henry VIII to give to Anne Boleyn in 1531 in exchange for Bromehill Priory, Norfolk. Income from this was missing, presumably, because Henry had plundered nearly all ecclesiastical establishments at the Dissolution of Monasteries etc. It was supposed to pay £20 a year to the college but it was nearly always in arrears. Hence gift of Manor and Parsonage of Bourn by Edward VI.

Lady Margaret Beaufort's Arms over the Master's Lodge, Christ's College. The Arms incorporate numerous daisies, or "marguerites", which she adopted as her emblem. Also in evidence is the Beaufort portcullis.

to provide water for both Emmanuel and Christ's Colleges. It still flows in the special 'runs' in the streets and it still fills the beautiful eighteenth century bathing pool in the college grounds.

Overlooking the bathing pool is the college's most famous member, the poet Milton. The statue of him, which stands among the bushes, is somewhat weathered and fails to do him credit. Milton was, in a sense, all things. He has been listed as an English poet, as a pamphleteer, scholar, theologian, historian and civil servant. Although from Oxfordshire stock he came to Cambridge at the age of sixteen when he entered Christ's. He remained for seven years until he achieved his M.A. degree in 1632. Milton fits rather neatly into the pattern we have seen, in which traditional forms of learning were beginning to undergo a period of drastic change. He disagreed with the traditional and medieval system of learning by disputation or a form of contest by words in which knowledge, attitude and ability were sharpened. Like Bacon he favoured more modern methods of study and at first was unpopular with both his tutor and other undergraduates. In due course these differences were settled and he became a personage of some standing within the college, as with the hindsight of time, we might expect. It was customary to write eulogies in Latin about various dignitaries — it might be regarded as comparable to the public relations exercise of the day — and this Milton did with much skill. Even the Latin exercises composed for his degrees still survive and these reveal a passionate, idealistic nature with a degree of forcefulness yet innocence which was to reveal itself in his later works. There were two outbreaks of plague while Milton was at the college. The place was kept shut and only Fellows were allowed out without permission. Apparently the traditional college retreat, the village of Malton, was no longer in use at this time.

Darwin, author of *Origin of the Species* was also at Christ's. He was soon known as "the man who walks with Henslow", the latter being the Professor of Botany. After his famous voyage in the *Beagle* to the Galapagos at which his ideas for the *Origin* really began to clarify themselves, he returned to Christ's as a Fellow Commoner while working up his results. Christ's College remains a particularly beautiful place and is undoubtedly one of Lady Margaret Beaufort's finer achievements. Financial resources were considerably improved in the early nineteenth century when coprolite, or fossilised dung which was of great value as a fertiliser, was found on Christ's College property. It yielded £21,500 in twenty years. I mention this just to emphasise the variety of ingredients which go to make aristocratic success or appalling failure in the life of something as changeable as a collegiate foundation!

Even if one had no idea that the Lady Margaret Beaufort was responsible for both Christ's and St John's Colleges there is a method by which the keen-eyed observer could tell. At both colleges the Master's Lodge possesses some superb heraldic carving on an oriel window. Each example contains Lady Margaret's arms and each is liberally covered with carved daisies, her personal

The Master's bell pull, Jesus College. A notice proclaims that it is worked by electricity and that it is not to be pulled unless an answer is required.

The large initials on the end of St John's College library commemorate John Williams, Bishop of Lincoln, who paid for its construction. They stand for *Johannes Lincolniensis Custos Sigilli.*

rebus or insignia. The same arms are to be seen over the main gateway and here again there is the Tudor Rose, the Beaufort portcullis and the innumerable daisies. Apparently she adopted this device because its French form, "Marguerite" represented her Christian name. There are other similarities between the founding of St John's and Christ's. In the case of the latter it was Byngham who was taken over. At St John's it was not just an individual, but an entire hospital.

Again, Fisher was very much the moving force and there is some evidence that a plan to convert the Hospital of St John into a college was being discussed with the Lady Margaret and her council as early as 1505. Lady Margaret did get as far as entering into some preliminary agreements about the change but when she died on June 29th 1509 her Will and intentions were far from complete. Fisher carried the plan through, sometimes after much difficulty, and procured papal, royal and episcopal licences for the dissolution of the hospital and the foundation of the college. As a result on March 12th 1511, a strange sight was to be seen on one of the quaysides which characterised the Cambridge river at that time. All the patients at the former hospital were gathered together and placed in a boat. They were taken to Ely. Only a few weeks earlier 800,000 bricks had been ordered from Richard Reculver of Greenwich, so there was little chance of a reprieve.

The old hospital chapel was restored for college use, while in St John's Lane the hospital infirmary was used first as a stable and then as a storehouse.

67

Marshy ground lay towards the river and beyond this, over a wooden bridge, were the hospital fishponds. We know that the college retained the ponds for some time, for when David Loggan came to make his famous engravings of Cambridge colleges the fishponds were clearly illustrated. In the early documents of St John's we can get some more interesting glimpses of just what college life must have been like during this period of the sixteenth century. Fellows and scholars shared the same room. In each chamber was a high bed for the Fellow and a low truckle bed for one or even two scholars. The living together of Fellows and pupils lasted for a considerable time after this, but however badly off the students were at this time, there were others who were to experience worse conditions. There is the story of Dr James Wood (1760 - 1839) who as a student occupied a garret just off 'O' staircase. He was too poor to afford a fire or even a light in his room and it is said that he used to study in the evenings with his feet wrapped in straw to protect them from the cold. The rush candle which lit the stairs was his only source of light. He was a brilliant man in spite of all this and his works on mathematics were standard material for many years. He eventually became a Fellow and Tutor at the college and its Master in 1815. His ghost is still supposed to haunt the staircase in which he suffered so much discomfort and it is reputed to have been seen on a number of occasions.

The poet Wordsworth was at St John's. Curiously enough his career at the college is generally considered to have been very ordinary and undistinguished. After taking his degree he decided not to enter a profession and spent a year in France, which turned out to be the most catastrophic of the Revolution. Later when he settled in England with his sister, the Cambridge influence appeared again in the form of Coleridge who, as we have seen, was at Jesus.

There is much that one could say about St John's college as a collection of buildings. It possesses one of the finest Combination Rooms in Cambridge, while its bridge over the river, a form of replica of the famous Bridge of Sighs, is photographed regularly by many visitors. It also has one of the most exciting pieces of new building in Cambridge - the Cripps building. This has been laid out like a continuous but bent ribbon in such a way that it provides three distinct courts. The river has been cleverly worked into the entire concept with the result that St John's now has its own 'punt park' leading off the Cam. The Cripps building extends from the old part of the college to the School of Pythagorus, a building older still. This was part of Merton Hall, owned until recent years by Merton College, Oxford. The building is late twelfth century Norman in parts and has recently been converted to form a hall for music and drama with an area below for entertaining.

One wonders what Fellows of the college from years past would have made of it all. Theirs was a curious life which reflected itself in most colleges of the time. It wasn't until 1861, for example, that the compulsion upon a Fellow to

A fine riverside setting for the Master's Lodge, St John's.

take Holy Orders was removed. Marriage was also a bar to Fellowships, for at that time the Fellows consisted largely of a body of celibate clergy. If they departed into matrimony they relinquished their Fellowship, but the college provided them with a neat way out by offering Livings in a number of Parishes which it possessed throughout the country.

A typical undergraduate's room at Cambridge.

CHAPTER NINE

Magdalene and Trinity

UNTIL quite recent times there was only one college on the north side of the river Cam. This was Magdalene, a small college even today and one which had been refounded from an earlier and almost destitute Foundation called Buckinham College. No longer is there any reason for Magdalene to feel out in the cold. The northern banks are now shared with such establishments as Girton, New Hall, Fitzwilliam College and if one goes round to the west a little, Selwyn, Darwin, Churchill and others.

Even so, Magdalene is the first college one comes to as one crosses what used to be the "Great Bridge" leading from the City to the north and west. The college is not very conspicuous and it is doubtful if the many visitors to the City are enticed inside by mere appearance. If the newcomer is knowledgeable, he will immediately turn in through the main gate and go in search of the Pepys building, for Magdalene College has been the owner of the famous Samuel Pepys diaries and papers ever since they were bequeathed to it in 1724. Pepys' library is still contained in his own bookcases and although one can be precise about when the books first arrived at the college there is less that can be said in the way of dates about the building which contains them.

In fact we cannot be certain of the architect. No records have come down to us about the beginning or the conclusion of the actual building although a letter of November 29th, 1670 to Pepys from John Maulyverer, a Fellow of the college says, "We have not yet finished the inside, and I know not when we shall." Pepys' library itself is contained in twelve bookcases of red oak which are believed to be those referred to by Pepys himself in his diary when he wrote "then comes Sympson to set up my other new presses for my books." The bookcases are all identical and all have glazed doors. Matching the cases is Pepys' flat-topped pedestal writing desk which also has glazed doors and rather rich mouldings.

However, in talking about Pepys we have rather jumped ahead of the origins of the college itself. It was from a series of representations made to Henry VI that monks from Crowland Abbey (sometimes known as Croyland) were sent to Cambridge to study canon law and theology. There was no hostel for the Benedictine order in the town with the result that the monks had to lodge with seculars and townspeople. The Abbot obtained letters patent for the establishment of a suitable hostel in two houses on the site of the present college and also hit upon a novel scheme for continuing the building and spreading the actual cost; other Benedictine houses in East Anglia were called upon to build a room each

The Pepys Building at Magdalene houses the **original** books and manuscripts of the famous diarist.

and thus Ely, Ramsey and Saffron Walden each took their share, although the college was still considered to be under the direct control of Crowland.

Two Dukes of Buckingham, Henry the second and Edward the third duke had each offered so much patronage and assistance to the new establishment that the college came to bear their name. Right up until the Dissolution of the Monasteries the little college remained in operation but a financial crisis was not far off and when, in 1542, Lord Audley of Saffron Walden stepped in and refounded it, the college had nearly ceased to exist. Thomas Audley of Walden was Lord Chancellor at the time and a man who was clearly in a position of some considerable influence. His Foundation dates from 1542 but he died in 1544 and in 1546 the records tell us that again the little college was in financial trouble. Queen Elizabeth visited Cambridge in 1546 and on that occasion Thomas Howard, fourth Duke of Norfolk, Audley's son-in-law and great grandson of Edward, third Duke of Buckingham, promised the college £40 a year towards completion of the first court. It sounds a small amount by modern standards but at that time it must have come like manna from heaven to the hard pressed Fellows. Originally Magdalen was spelled without the final 'e' like its counterpart at Oxford and there is no definite record of the change being made. However in the eighteenth century the college became associated with the Evangelical movement of the period to the extent that it became its centre and it has been suggested that it took up the final 'e', not only to distinguish it from the Oxford version but to bring it into line with Biblical usage. The exact date of this change is uncertain but it must lie between 1816 and 1820 for it is at this point that the new spelling occurs in the University Almanack of the day.

In addition to Pepys, Magdalene College has had other famous men through its doors. Charles Kingsley, author of *The Water Babies* graduated in 1842, while the Archbishop of Canterbury, Dr A.M. Ramsey and Marshal of the Royal Air Force Lord Tedder are more recent names to go on the records.

Originally the college grounds were on the north of the river and the east of Magdalene Street, but in recent years the college has developed property across the road to a considerable extent. Now it must be one of the few Cambridge colleges with a main road, Magdalene Street, running through it. However much they may differ in terms of size, constitution, wealth and position, all Cambridge colleges are laid out to the same basic formulae of entrances, courts, hall, chapel and so on. Magdalene managed to reflect this with some skill in its modern development at Benson Court across the road.

Trinity College. The Wren Library.

Trinity College might follow Magdalene historically, but it is at the opposite end of the pole in everything else. It is one of the largest colleges in physical terms and indeed the main court is the biggest in the city. Its' position of power and influence is unrivalled and the famous men who have passed through its gates would make a very large volume in themselves. It was founded by Henry VIII as one of the last acts of his life and its Royal associations have remained paramount ever since. One cannot really escape Henry as one wanders round the college. His statue gazes down from the gate towers and stands masterfully, hands on hips, staring from a large painting in the magnificent dining hall. Trinity still has Royal associations; it is the only Cambridge college for which the Master is appointed by the Crown, the college flag is in fact the flag of Edward III, and when the judges appointed by the monarch visited the Cambridge Assizes they always resided in the ground floor of the Master's Lodge. This ancient privilege dated from the reign of James I and was always willingly accepted by the college, even though the judges had no legal right. The disappearance of the Assizes from Cambridge in 1971, largely due to the lack of suitable Assize Courts, brought to end the colourful ceremonies in which the Judge's trumpeters always heralded his arrival and departure.

It was typical of Henry VIII that he absorbed two other colleges into his spectacular last minute effort. These were King's Hall (quite distinct incidentally from King's College founded by Henry VI) and Michaelhouse. Henry had recently completed the dissolution of the monasteries and in founding his college he gave it a considerable amount of confiscated wealth in addition to the land and property of King's Hall and Michaelhouse. The latter college never survived although there are some of its stones in the south west corner of the Great Court. King's Hall was different and it was from this college that Trinity obtained the two very fine gateways of the college as it stands today. The Great Gate, which represents the main entrance from Trinity Street dates back to 1490 and once marked the entrance to the grounds of King's Hall. It is a splendid affair and on it is the statue of Henry VIII holding a chairleg and beneath him the name of Edward III, founder of King's Hall, and the coats of arms of his sons. Several attempts have been made to equip Henry with a decent sceptre to go with the orb he holds in his left hand, but agile undergraduates always replace the chairleg as soon as the sun goes down. Now the chairleg is part of the scene and Trinity main gate and Henry would seem strange without it.

The other gateway which the college inherited is on the north side of the Great Court. This is in fact a clock tower and was built as the gateway of King's Hall between 1428 and 1432. It too has had an interesting career, for when Thomas Neville, the Master in 1615, swept away a number of older buildings to create the present Great Court he found that the tower ruined his overall concept by its prominent position. To overcome this he had the entire tower

Great Court, Trinity, the largest college court at either Oxford or Cambridge. In the foreground stands the Elizabethan fountain. Behind is the Edward III tower which once stood on the spot marked by the sundial visible in front of it. It was moved back stone by stone when Dr Thomas Neville reshaped the court in the sixteenth century.

moved back twenty yards stone by stone to its present site. The clock is the same timepiece described by Wordsworth as "loquacious" in his famous Prelude and it is a further tradition of Trinity that undergraduates regularly attempt to race round the entire court when it is striking midnight. Their task is a difficult one, for the Court measures 287ft 6 inches (south side), 344ft 5 inches (west), 256ft 6 inches (north) and 325ft 7 inches (east) enclosing a total area of 79,059 feet! Mathematicians and athletes can work out the distances and times for themselves.

Neville not only created this huge and impressive Court but he also played a large part in the neighbouring Neville's Court which now bears his name. Such was his enthusiasm that he built two thirds of the cloisters in this very Italianate setting with his own private resources. The urge to work on this particular court seems to have been strong in others, for Sir Christopher Wren, who created the library building with its piazza beneath, also gave his services. This is undoubtedly to the letter, according to Wren's original drawings for it which are preserved at All Souls College, Oxford. The only change of plan lay in the positioning of the building which was ultimately set 27 yards further west than originally intended. To cope with this the sides of Neville's Court were extended to meet it. So strong is the Italianate impression created by the finished scheme that it is sometimes difficult to realise that one is in Cambridge as one walks round the piazza and the broad cloisters on either side.

Not all Masters of Trinity were as generous or as well liked as Neville. In the chapel is a stone to Richard Bentley and from a casual glance there is nothing on it to indicate to the visitor that Bentley was a Master of the college. This is

Newton's apple tree, Trinity. This small tree, planted in 1954 beneath rooms once occupied by Newton, is descended from an apple tree at Woolsthorpe Manor, Yorkshire, traditionally associated with his discovery of the theory of gravitation.

because he was about to be deprived of the office when he died. Bentley became Master in 1700 and the story of his clash with other members of the college and the Fellows indicates rather graphically the manner in which the head of a college could profoundly influence its fortunes. Bentley has been described as both great and mean. His bad relationships and emnities with others began to affect the prospects of pupils and he was also cursed with "greed and truculence." Eventually he was accused of misdemeanours of varying sorts by the Fellows and he found himself before the Court of the Bishop of Ely who acted as independent arbitrator or Visitor to the college. It was said that he had used college property to his own private ends and that he had deliberately thwarted the education of his opponents' sons and relatives. On two occasions the decision of the Bishop's court went against him but he was saved, almost miraculously, by the death of the Bishop on one occasion and by the refusal of the Vice Chancellor to carry out a sentence of deprivation of the Mastership. He was still Master when he died, but the fact that the Court had ordered him to relinquish the position weighed heavily with the Fellows. They saw to it that he received no recognition on his tombstone.

One cannot talk of personalities at Trinity without referring to Newton, the man who in my opinion had one of the greatest brains of any human being. He spent all his academic life from 1661 to 1696 at the college and his rooms were just to the right of the Great Gate on the first floor, staircase E.4. Newton calculated the basic laws of motion and physics by which all today's modern rocketry and space travel are carried out, although this did not spring from being hit upon the head by an apple as is popularly supposed. An apple did play some part in his thinking as Newton himself recorded in a conversation with his friend William Stukeley. In his *Memoirs of Sir Isaac Newton's Life* Stukeley recalls, "After dinner, the weather being warm, we went into the garden and drank thea, only he and myself. Amidst other discourse, he told me, he was just in the same situation, as when formerly the notion of gravitation came into his mind. It was occasioned by the fall of an apple, as he sat in contemplative mood. Why should that apple always descend perpendicularly to the ground, thought he to himself. Why should it not go sideways or upwards, but constantly to the earth's centre?" The part played by the apple has not been overlooked by Trinity College, for on the right hand side of the main entrance in what was once Newton's garden, an apple tree was planted in 1954. It was no ordinary apple tree either, for it was a direct descendant from the one at Newton's home at Woolsthorpe Manor, near Grantham, traditionally associated with the incident he described to his friend. Newton's great work *Principia Mathematica of 1687* is in the Wren Library at the college. The version which is particularly interesting is an early edition with Newton's own modifications and additions in his own handwriting. This is occasionally put on display in the library where visitors may inspect it through a glass case. The library also has a small pocketbook begun by Newton when he first moved to Cambridge and from this we know that he paid two shillings and **twopence** for "a chamberpot" and a further two shillings for "a Stilton."

Other Trinity men include Lord Byron, Bacon, Alfred Lord Tennyson, John Dryden and many others. Byron lived in Neville's Court and in a letter to a lady friend dated from Trinity College refers to the bear which he kept whilst at Cambridge; "I have got a new friend, the finest in the world, a tame bear. When I brought him here, they asked me what I meant to do with him, and my reply was 'he should sit for a fellowship.' This answer delighted them not. We have several parties here, and this evening a large assortment of jockies, gamblers, boxers, authors, parsons and poets." It sounded a very jolly and cosmopolitan function, but Byron did not keep his bear in the college as is sometimes said. Usually it was housed nearby at Ram Yard. The statue of Byron by Thorwaldsen which dominates the interior of the Wren Library was originally offered to Westminster Abbey but tactfully turned down by the Dean on the grounds that Byron had been too immoral.

Above this statue is a curious window of coloured glass dating from the reign of George III. It shows Fame presenting Newton to George III whilst Bacon makes notes in the background.

James I at Trinity. This statue of James I with his wife, left, and his son, Prince Charles (afterwards Charles I) was placed on the Great Gate to commemorate a visit.

CHAPTER TEN

Emmanuel and Sidney Sussex

A MERICANS are among the most enthusiastic visitors to Cambridge. There is the story of one who became thoroughly annoyed at the absence of labels on college buildings and eventually knocked on a handsome front door. It was answered by a stately butler who listened as the visitor asked, "Is this a college?". The butler replied that it was, and that he happened to be at the Master's Lodge. "Then why don't you have a sign up or something," the American asked. The butler drew himself up to his not inconsiderable height and replied, "Sir. This is Pembroke College - not Pembroke and Co."

I always feel that it would have been more appropriate had the visitor arrived at Emmanuel College instead. There he would not only have found the word "Emmanuel" incorporated in the college crest and coat of arms, but he would also have discovered a very definite connection with America. Of the one hundred and thirty men who emigrated from English Universities to New England before 1646, no less than a hundred were from Cambridge, and of these thirty five were from Emmanuel. Among the early pioneers from the college were Simon Bradstreet, the first Governor of Massachusetts, Daniel Denison, Major General of the colonial forces, Thomas Hooker, a notable exponent of primitive Congregationalism and John Harvard, benefactor of the American University which carries his name. Harvard entered Emmanuel College in 1627 and emigrated in 1637 only to die in the following year.

The reason for this mass exodus to the United States is to be found in the off-centre religious views which tended to have their focal point at Emmanuel. Puritanism had its home at the college while one can also trace Congregationalism, Presbyterianism and other religious developments at various times throughout the centuries. Typical of the Puritan influence at the college is the interesting history of the present dining hall, which was formerly the library and before that, the chapel. As was appropriate to Puritan notions the chapel ran north and south, not east and west, and they saw to it that it was never consecrated. Later when views changed no less a person than Sir Christopher Wren was commissioned to design the present chapel which stands opposite the main entrance and is set in the more conventional east-west position.

There was never any doubt about Emmanuel's religious purpose, right from the earliest days. The founder was Sir Walter Mildmay, Chancellor of the Exchequer to Elizabeth the First, and like Jesus College which occupied the site of a former nunnery, Emmanuel was established on the land of a former monastery. Mildmay took the view that the study of theology in the University had much decayed and his chief aim in establishing the college was to provide a steady supply of educated clergy for the reformed church. Part of the college fabric extends back to this period, and is incorporated in the Hall which, in the case of Emmanuel, must not be confused with the dining hall.

Mildmay had established his college at a time when the earlier patterns of teaching and scholastic life at Cambridge were beginning to settle down and adopt the shape they were to retain for the next century or so. It was about this time that the "Grace Books" or account books of the University itself ceased to refer to the systems of hostels to which we referred in earlier chapters. Now all students were housed within their college, many of which had undertaken large expansion schemes to cope with increased popularity and numbers. Not only did the college buildings increase in number but they also improved in splendour, an indication of the growing stature and importance of such establishments. After the foundation of Sidney Sussex, the next college to be established after Emmanuel, the total number of colleges at Cambridge (then sixteen) remained exactly the same until the arrival of Downing College in the comparatively recent year of 1800.

Similar changes had taken place in the methods of teaching. In the Middle Ages this had depended, largely on lectures given by such individuals as Regent Masters but by the fifteenth century some colleges were beginning to offer instruction to their members themselves. Then came the decline in numbers during the sixteenth century which had the effect of cutting back the fees the Regent Masters might expect, while growth of the colleges themselves at a slightly later date led to them taking a more active share in teaching than ever before. It was at about this time that the Regius Professorships were first formed and the holders of these titles or "chairs" came to be responsible for much higher standards of instruction, while the simpler work, which had been carried out under the Regents, was now the task of the college tutor.

Soon the tutor was to occupy the important and integral part of Cambridge college life which has been his up to the present day. He has been described thus, "a fellow of the college is to be responsible for his pupil's expenses, to explain to him what he has to do and to learn, and, in return, is to be treated by him with filial obedience and respect." With the possible exception of the filial obedience and respect, this is very much the role of the tutor today. In addition to seeing a pause in college founding, after the arrival of Sidney Sussex, the sixteenth century saw other changes. Until this time the University and its colleges had been primarily concerned with the provision of clerics, as we have seen with the foundation of Corpus Christi, Emmanuel and others. Now the sons of noblemen began to arrive at Cambridge and as one might expect, their ideas and their requirements differed. They were looking for training which would fit them as men of affairs and gradually alterations and dispensations in various sets of statutes evolved in order to cope with the change.

Sir Christoper Wren's Chapel at Emmanuel College.

But the fact remains that the colleges founded at this period had a distinctly religious background nonetheless. Sidney Sussex, which brought new colleges at Cambridge to an end for a period of two hundred years, was no exception. As in the case of Jesus College, it represented the establishment of an academic foundation on the site of a former religious institution. The site, between Jesus Lane and Sidney Street, was formerly occupied by Franciscan Friars who had settled there in the thirteenth century and had built their church, cloisters and friary. All this came to an ignominious end when Henry VIII suppressed the monasteries and it was not long before the King had granted the Friars' establishment to Trinity College.

Henry's college of Trinity used a considerable quantity of stones and materials and most of the Friary buildings were destroyed. When one stands in the

Great Court at Trinity and looks at the walls one is in reality looking at the same masonry which was used in this earlier religious establishment.

In the meantime Lady Frances Sidney, Countess of Sussex, had nursed the idea of founding an educational establishment at Cambridge in memory of her late husband, the Earl of Sussex. When she died in 1589 she was buried in Westminster Abbey and her will revealed that she had set aside £5,000 for the college project. She had also had a special piece of jewellery made up which her executors were to take to the King when they sought his permission for a new Foundation. On the jewel was a hand delivering up a heart to a crown with a "humble suit" in her name for the establishment of a college. Eventually Henry did give his assent and the site of "The Lady Frances Sidney Sussex College", as Lady Sidney called it, was transferred to her executors.

The building that was to be built on this site, in a period of three years it is said, illustrates very well the way in which different men from different ages altered in their tastes and feelings towards architecture. A little *Traveller's Guide to Cambridge* published in 1888 says of Sidney Sussex, "This college has such a modern appearance from having been faced throughout with cement within the last forty years; previous to this great alteration it was a gloomy, irregular pile of the later Elizabethan period in red brick and stone...." When in 1960 the Royal Commission on Historical Monuments came to look at the same college it commented, "At Sidney Sussex college the drabness of the buildings belies the qualities evident in the early nineteenth century drawings of them."! These days we are inclined to regard Elizabethan brickwork as something beautifully toned, soft and mellow. The idea of plastering wet cement all over it tends to fill us with horror. Perhaps the next century or so will see further changes of taste; Sidney Sussex and other colleges like it may yet be faced with weatherproof plastic!

One of the important days in the history of Sidney Sussex was April 23rd 1616. It was then that a young man, not yet seventeen, was admitted as a Fellow Commoner. His name was Oliver Cromwell. The college books duly recorded "Oliverus Cromwell Huntingdoniensus admissus ad commeatum siciorum Aprilis vicesimo secto, tutore Mag^o Ricardo Howlet." Much later, and presumably after Cromwell had managed to turn England upside down and plunge it into Civil War, another hand wrote in the book, "Grandis impostor; carnifax perditissimus" etc., etc! Cromwell did not stay long at the college. He was obliged to leave after one year because of the death of his father. Unfortunately no record has come down to us of his stay at the college other than his name in the entry lists and the note of the sale, amongst other plate, of a piece of silver which he presented to the college on his admission. It is unlikely that this gesture was a signal of his beneficence and good intent. Many colleges insisted that newcomers presented them with a piece of silver or something similar as a means of increa-

Sidney Sussex seen from Sidney Street.

sing their wealth, and Sidney Sussex have been no exception. Curiously enough when Civil War did break out the college, like many others at Cambridge, supported the King and sent £100 for his use. Unlike other colleges however, there is no record of them sending silver. The thought of Oliver's piece going towards the opposing cause would have been ironic to say the least.

Sidney Sussex has one other distinction, that of being the first Cambridge college to admit a Scotsman as a Fellow. Originally when its Statutes were laid down, Fellows of the college were to be Englishmen and poor students were to be given a definite preference. In due course the limitation to English nationality was rescinded and Fellowships became open to Scotsmen and Irishmen provided they had studied for six years at Cambridge. Shortly before this, John Young, said to be the first Scotsman to ever take a degree in the University, was elected a Fellow of the college in 1606. He later became Dean of Winchester. It was absolutely essential that Master and Fellows were to be very pure in their religion and opposed to Popery and other heresies. Students were only admitted to the college if they were of "virtuous life and unsullied reputation." The standards were clearly well kept, for when the notorious William Dowsing visited Sidney Sussex in 1643 he reported, "We saw nothing there to be amended."

It would be a mistake to assume that colleges these days are concerned purely with the creature comforts and needs of their members. Sidney Sussex, like many Cambridge colleges, looks after large numbers of visitors who arrive in Cambridge during the Long Vacation to take part in Summer Schools, Symposia and various forms of conference and teaching. The Catering Manager for the college tells me that he can recall a time when a college would virtually close down for the summer months. Many of the kitchen staff would be laid off completely only to be re-engaged when the summer vacation ended and the college was about to burst into life again. Now the picture is totally different. It is important to a college that it continues to receive an income from capital equipment and new buildings in which it may have invested heavily. Sidney Sussex overhauled the kitchens and catering arrangements in 1948 - 50 when new designs were prepared by Basil Ward. Now the catering staff remain in employment all the year round and accommodation at the college is put to good use when the undergraduates have gone down for the summer. Recently the college undertook a spectacular piece of reconstruction when the entire interior of the Sir Francis Clerke range of buildings was removed and the interior layout totally revised. As a result some of the medieval lavatory arrangements, which always surprised visitors, were removed and conditions generally were made more comfortable for anyone staying at the college during the summer months. Other colleges at Cambridge have undertaken similar schemes. Conferences and visiting institutions of all kinds have come to play their part in the economics of college housekeeping in a manner which would have been unimaginable in years gone by.

CHAPTER ELEVEN

Nineteenth and Twentieth Century Colleges

DOWNING College must be our stepping stone into the present day. Of course it is not modern in the sense of New Hall, Churchill College or even Girton, but it does form the half-way link with that great period of college development which ended with Sidney Sussex. The buildings of Downing have a strangely ageless air about them, styled as they are in the Ionic Order and set around an enormous and spacious site. Where other colleges of more venerable age jostle each other in the city centre, Downing luxuriates in more than enough space for its needs. The large open quadrangle formed by the present buildings is still open to the south. A wing to close this gap was once planned but has never been built.

Several legal actions lay between Downing and its very existence. Had it not been for an outcome successful to the University, the college might never have existed at all. Sir George Downing of Gamlingay Hall in Cambridgeshire left a number of valuable estates to his relatives with the additional clause that should they all die without issue the money was to go to trustees who were to found a college at Cambridge called Downing College. In due course the sole inheritor left the estates to his wife which were then promptly claimed by the University. The legal battle lasted many years but eventually the University was successful and the first stone was laid on May 18th 1807 and the college admitted its first under-graduates in 1821.

William Wilkins, the architect for the new college, has provided Cambridge with an excellent example of the revived Greek style which was popular at the time, just before it plunged into darkest Victoriana with Selwyn College and Girton. The use of large areas of grass and lawn against the almost soothing form-ality of the Greek style has produced a scene with an almost idyllic quality about it. Wilkins succeeded because he ignored the traditional college plan and knew what he was going to put in its stead. Selwyn and Girton did not find themselves in such an adventurous period, architecturally speaking. Selwyn, situated far beyond the University Library tower and the Backs, possesses the formal and traditional ground plan. There was a period when it was fashionable to have a good laugh at the expense of Selwyn because of its architecture, and a smile at Girton because it represented the first Cambridge incursion into the realms of higher education for women. Now both facets have changed; Victoriana is attracting an increasing number of admirers, while Girton, never short of admirers, must represent a hallowed bastion in the movement for Women's Liberation.

Even so, when the Royal Commission on Historical Monuments came to look at Selwyn in the 1960's they could not see anything in the buildings that they

Downing College.

considered worth preserving. Like Girton it does not rate a mention in the famous report! If we adhere to a strictly chronological order for the later Cambridge colleges we should bring Newnham, the second women's college, into the picture at this point. Newnham also favoured red brick and an abundance of pinewood and stained glass windows when the present buildings were begun in 1880. However its founders were not quite so concerned about the problems of bringing young women into man's preserve as was Emilie Davies, the doughty originator and founder of Girton. Emilie Davies would brook no changes in the educational standards it was proposed to provide for women. Her girls had to have the same degrees and examinations to work for as anyone else. But in social attitude she was more conventional and her original establishment was sited as far away from Cambridge as Hitchin in the hope that the more enthusiastic undergraduates would tire a little before pursuing the girls over a total distance of twenty six miles. Even when the college was eventually moved to Cambridge it was she who insisted that the establishment should be at Girton. Generations of Girton girls, walking and cycling that interminable distance along the Huntingdon Road, have both blessed and cursed her for it ever since!

As we have seen Newnham was not affected by similar qualms. The site, just off Sidgewick Avenue, is remarkably convenient compared with Girton. Secluded, yes, but within walking distance of everything that matters. It was the North of England Council for Promoting the Higher Education of Women which was directly responsible for founding the college. The Council was concerned about the low intellectual standards in girls' schools towards the latter end of the nineteenth century and eventually succeeded in promoting suitable examinations and courses for them at Cambridge. In 1871 the first vital steps towards establishing a group of women students in Cambridge were taken and five were admitted to a house in Regent Street. The same year the University first formally recognised Newnham and Girton colleges and opened the Tripos examinations to their women students. Degrees for women, however, were another story and it was not until the 1920's that full degrees were available to women at Cambridge.

As its name suggests, New Hall is the newcomer, certainly as far as women's colleges are concerned. Its present buildings on the Huntingdon Road by Chamberlin, Powell and Bon are startling in their originality. Probably the most striking object is the central dome which stands out white against the sky. I was once earnestly informed by a newcomer to Cambridge that it was the site of the University's astronomical observatories. He was surprised when he learned the true nature of the building and had to journey round to Madingley Road to

"Traditional forms used in an up to date manner"—Selwyn College development for graduates and undergraduates at Cranmer Road.

assure himself that the true astronomical domes housing telescopes were really there!

Like Girton, New Hall sprang from a small body of people who were anxious to establish a college for women. The need co-incided with the University's moves in 1948 to admit more women. Like Newnham it originated from a small Association which in the early days provided itself with premises in Silver Street, Cambridge for a short while, and in common with the foundation of all Cambridge colleges, it faced a pressing need to accumulate sufficient funds to provide suitable endowments. Some of the existing colleges for men were most generous. King's College, for example, gave considerable help to the newcomer and so did St John's. Other funds came from outside organisations of a most varied nature, girls' schools for example, and even the Soroptimists. It was not until 1967 however that all the college's members were housed in their present splendid and controversial buildings.

Red brick at Cambridge. Selwyn College, main gate.

Girton, the first Cambridge College for women. The main gate.

Newnham College main entrance with the Mistress's residence on the left.

Immediately next door to New Hall is Fitzwilliam. This too has an impressive new building and was given full collegiate status in 1960, the same year as Churchill College also officially came into being. Here, however, the similarity ends. Churchill College is the only establishment of its type to have been completely planned and brought into being in its entirety since the war. Fitzwilliam had been in Cambridge in a tangible and recognisable form for about a hundred years, but as a community rather than a full college.

There was something distinctly medieval about the evolution of Fitzwilliam. The reader will recall that when scholars first began to arrive in Cambridge they did not attach themselves to a college and in fact lived in lodgings or hostels. Following the Royal Commission on Oxford and Cambridge in 1850 the idea of a reversion to first principles of this nature gained ground. It was hoped that by such a device a University education would become available to many people who were unable to afford the high college fees charged at the time. The suggestion was not welcomed by existing colleges but nevertheless some non-collegiate students, as they were known, did arrive in Cambridge under the auspices of a Non-Collegiate Students Board. Inevitably the non-collegiate students banded together and began to form their own clubs and institutions. Eventually some rooms were obtained at a house in Trumpington Street which was opposite the Fitzwilliam Museum. The new body called itself Fitzwilliam House and even got permission to use Lord Fitzwilliam's arms in a coat of its own. Evolution was gradual. Dining in hall became the norm, a chapel was established and Fitzwilliam swelled in numbers.

Eventually the finance was found to provide new buildings on the Huntingdon Road and in 1966 the University took the view that Fitzwilliam had the resources and the standing to take on full college status.

At about the same time Churchill College was evolving but in a very much different way. Churchill is not far from New Hall and Fitzwilliam, geographically speaking. A brief cycle ride along the Huntingdon Road and left into Storey's Way and there stands a piece of architecture which is admired by some and heavily criticised by others. However, one has a right to expect that Sir Winston Churchill was in some way involved in its inception, and this was indeed the case. His personal preference for innovators, rather than people who were simply nice, led him to realise that it was scientific skills which would contribute more to the well-being of the country in the future rather than any basic military power, which in any case was a non-starter. He and Lord Cherwell considered a number

Newnham College, the new wing.

New Hall. The Dining Hall.

Fitzwilliam College, designed by Denys Lasdun and Partners.

of ideas to ensure that the country's supply of scientists and technologists would not fail. In principle it was much the same thought which prompted the Guilds of Corpus and Christi to become concerned about the availability of a sufficient number of prayers for their souls although the ultimate application was to be a little different. Sir Winston and his advisers found that there was not much enthusiasm among industrialists and others for a type of English Massachusetts Institute of Technology or even a post-graduate institute at Birmingham. But a new college at Cambridge. Now that was different!

It was an idea which produced a greater reaction and in no time the outline scheme was soon approved by the Cambridge Senate on February 13th 1958. A panel of trustees, led by Sir Winston himself, ran an architectural competition in two stages which was limited to the top twenty-one architects of the period. Four designs were selected for development in more detail and eventually that by Richard Sheppard of Richard Robson and Partners won the day. *Cambridge New Architecture* makes a very apposite comment on the present day appearance of the college. "Many critics have made the obvious comparison between the massive rough-hewn college and the massive rough-hewn hero it commemorates; 'informal but grand' in Banham's words 'not unlike the finest-hour image of the stout person in a siren suit' ".

93

The education factory. Concrete chimneys and sculpture by Henry Moore make a strange contrast at Churchill College.

Sir John Cockcroft, himself a most distinguished scientist was to become the first Master and soon the college began to receive a variety of gifts. General de Gaulle gave a fine tapestry, Dame Barbara Hepworth gave examples of her sculpture and the college also received works by Epstein and others. Walking around the grounds today one can see Barbara Hepworth's "Squares with two Circles" sited on the lawns, with works by Henry Moore nearby and also flanking the main entrance. Countries of the Commonwealth presented some fine timber panelling and the present college chapel was in large measure a gift from the Reverend Timothy Beaumont. Sir Winston Churchill, like Sir John Cockcroft, did not live to see the college far on its way. After Sir Winston's death it was learned that it was his intention that his books and papers and other documents of great historical importance to the country should be entrusted to the care of his college. This has now become the case and so the youngest of the Cambridge colleges, true to the tradition of so many others, has become the curator, so to speak, of part of our national heritage.

Churchill College. Residential block.

CHAPTER TWELVE

Graduate Colleges and other Institutions

THE DIFFERENCE between a full college within the University and that of a graduate college is relatively small and comparatively new. Cambridge now possesses a number of graduate colleges and similar bodies and already these are beginning to build up a community structure which one day could admit them to the university as full colleges within their own right. Basically a full membership of the university can only be granted to a body which is considered completely self-sufficient in the sense that it is financially independent and permanently endowed. An approved foundation, as these other institutions and graduate colleges are known, is not allowed to nominate Proctors of the University, and neither is it expected to pay an annual contribution to the University for the ten years following its official recognition. Similarly, the head of such a body is not eligible for nomination to hold the office of Vice Chancellor of the University.

A good example of an approved foundation which falls into this category is Darwin College, the first of the graduate colleges to be founded in recent years. Professor E.G. Young, the first Master of Darwin College, set out the thinking behind graduate colleges when he wrote an excellent short history of the college. "Its Foundation sprang from a growing realisation that the number of research students in residence in the University of Cambridge was likely to rise steadily during the forseeable future, and to rise relatively more rapidly than the number of undergraduates." These graduates, many of whom were also engaged in teaching, needed a focal point, a parent body which could provide them with the same sort of community background which formed the essence of a Cambridge college. Thus the need for a graduate college became more and more apparent.

Darwin College was really founded by the members of Gonville and Caius, St John's and Trinity Colleges who put up considerable sums of money to help it on its way. On December 31st, 1962, some six months before the proposal was accepted by the Council of the Senate, Sir Charles Darwin, the grandson of Charles Darwin who had written *The Evolution of the Species,* died. Many people now know his home, Newnham Grange and the Old Granary through that splendid little book *Period Piece* which was written by Sir Charles's sister, Gwen Raverat. On Sir Charles' death the rest of the family decided to move from Cambridge, and the Grange and Old Granary became available. In due course the premises were purchased for the new college and the family agreed to the suggestion that it should be named after that famous English naturalist, Darwin. Later still, a house named The Hermitage, standing on the corner of Silver Street and Newnham

Darwin College. The Old Granary from the Mill Pool.

Terrace was bought and now the whole of this area has been welded into one effective collegiate unit by the architects Howell, Killick, Partridge and Amis.

Visitors to Darwin will almost certainly note the beautiful old Granary which stands by the edge of the Mill Pool. Now it is all that remains of a once thriving commercial area of warehouses and docksides which stood on the spot. Anyone with a keen eye will note that it appears to tilt slightly. The Bursar of Darwin, Brigadier Arthur Stuart-Clark, himself an engineer, tells me that when investigations were made of the foundations of the Granary building it was found to be seated on a bed of interwoven rushes and canes. In spite of, or more probably because of this the building was perfectly secure and as sound as the day it was built.

Darwin College was the first of the graduate colleges, but by 1966 it had become one of a number. University College, Clare Hall and Lucy Cavendish college, all institutions of a similar structure, appeared on the scene. University College is particularly interesting for it is the only college or institution to be directly founded by the University itself. There were earlier attempts to persuade the University to support such an undertaking. University Hall, founded by Richard de Badew in 1326 was an example, but as we have seen financial problems eventually brought Lady Clare to incorporate it in Clare Hall. University College today is a graduate institution, like Darwin. The site was given by the University who also undertook to provide generous financial support for the first ten years of its existence.

Of course women have not been overlooked in this very modern trend towards graduate bodies of one sort or another. Lucy Cavendish College, which obtained its status as an approved society in 1965, is a graduate college for women only as one might reasonably expect from its rather charming name. The title is derived from that of Lady Lucy Cavendish who was sister to the well-known headmaster of Eton and a niece of Mr Gladstone. In common with some other distinguished women who helped found colleges at Cambridge, Lady Lucy devoted her long life to charitable, religious and educational causes. Two small cottages in Northampton Street provided the college with its first set of offices, but more recently it has acquired the lease of a large private house in Lady Margaret Road, a highly appropriate address. There it will continue to provide the social and community needs of its members.

Hughes Hall, another women's establishment, is intended for teacher training women graduates. It gained the status of a recognised institution in 1949 but it began in Cambridge many years before during the Victorian period. Those who took part in the original discussions for the foundation of the college, in Miss Clough's rooms at Newnham College in the 1880's, felt that there was a need for a college to look after the more technical aspects of women's teacher training. After a slow evolutionary history the college has moved from building to building, each time expanding a little and gaining in stature. Now it has an enviable site offering a fine view of the University Cricket and Sports Ground known as Fenner's.

Similar in character, although not quite of the same University status as yet, is Homerton College. It has fine grounds on the Hills Road and specialises in teacher training of women students. Its beginnings can be traced back to the Congregational Fund Board started in London in 1695 for the training of ministers. Homerton is now undenominational and its status continues to rise. Recently it put up students for the first Cambridge Bachelor of Education Degrees to be awarded to a non-university college. Forty Homerton girls were presented to the University for the degree by Newnham College and the total number of Homerton students with this new degree increases yearly.

Theological Colleges of varying denominations have long been established at Cambridge, but changes are taking place. Westcott House, Ridley Hall and Wesley House represent a blending together of two Anglican establishments with one Methodist college in a form of rationalisation which is now proposed. This does not mean that the three colleges will lose their individual identities. The new structure will take the form of a federation, with distinct advantages in economic terms and in organisation. Other ecclesiastical establishments have done the same. Cheshunt College, for example, which for many years occupied a fine building near the University Botanic Gardens has recently amalgamated with Westminster College. Like Cheshunt College, Westminster is a Presbyterian training college and occupies a splendid site at the end of Queen's Road on The Backs.

But for all its colleges, Cambridge shows no sign of running out of new foundations. Some of them come from the very oldest as in the case of Clare Hall. This is a daughter establishment of Clare College and takes the form of a residential foundation for visiting scholars and their families. Its buildings, designed by Ralph Erskine in a strictly Scandinavian idiom, are a unique blend of domestic needs, like houses and flats, incorporated into a working collegiate structure. Clare Hall is like a tiny academic suburb with children riding their bicycles and playing in narrow modern passageways and scholars working in the peace and quiet of specially positioned studies. Thus the corporate life of a college, so important in all Cambridge foundations, is retained alongside the needs of graduates and visiting scholars who bring their families with them and who require something totally different from the quiet courts of the traditional and celibate cleric.

Darwin College showing how Newnham Grange was incorporated into the new facade.

GLOSSARY

Chancellor .... Official head of the University. Is elected by the vote of the Senate and holds office until death or resignation.

Vice Chancellor .... Represents the University in the absence of the Chancellor which for all practical purposes is most everyday occasions. The Council of the Senate normally nominates two candidates, who must be heads of colleges, for this office. Traditionally the Regent House elects the senior man without taking a vote. Two years later at the end of the term of office the second candidate is elected, because he has now become the senior candidate.

The Senate .... The government of the University. All M.A.'s are members of the Senate. The Senate elects certain university officers and confers degrees. It also discusses reports, graces and other matters.

The Regent House .... Second tier of government. Consists of the graduate staffs of university and colleges in residence who meet before the gathering of the Senate every second Saturday throughout term. The Senior Proctor reads the graces and after each the junior Proctor shouts "placet" (agreed) unless a member shouts "non placet" (not agreed) before him. If this is called the Regent House must vote on the issue. Graces can only be put down by the Council of the Senate which consists of the Chancellor, the Vice Chancellor and sixteen members elected by the Regent House.

Grace .... A resolution or motion put before the Governing Houses.

Bachelor of Arts .... The most common degree to which graduates are admitted.

Master of Arts .... Whether resident or non-resident within the University the Bachelor of Arts may be admitted to the degree of Master of Arts six years after the end of his first term of residence. There is no examination but a fee of £3 is paid. The M.A. automatically becomes a member of the Regent House and thus obtains a share in the day to day government of the University.

Tripos .... In practice a degree with honours. Originally called Tripos because the examiner sat upon a three-legged stool. Normally an Honours Degree or Tripos is obtained by taking one specialised subject. The Honours degree can, however, be made up in certain circumstances of parts from different Triposes.

Master .... Head of a college, usually elected by the Fellows. Exceptions include King's College which has a Provost, and Queens' College which is headed by a President. The Mastership of Trinity is a Crown appointment, that of Magdalene is in the gift of the Barony of Braybrooke representing the founder, while that of Selwyn is elected by a Council containing a number of members from outside the college.

Scholar .... Normally a member of a college who, before coming into residence, has been elected to a scholarship on the result of an open competition conducted by the college.

Fellow .... Normally a B.A. or holder of a higher degree who has been elected to a Fellowship of a college with a view to teaching, administration or research. He receives a 'dividend' or share of the college income, is given rooms in college and is provided with dinner at the 'High' table.

Fellow Commoner .... Usually a young man of wealth or the younger son of nobility who had the privilege of dining at High Table. Other privileges enjoyed by them were the cause of much envy hence nicknames like "Licensed sons of ignorance."

Sizar .... Lowest student in the social hierarchy. In return for free 'commons' or food had to perform many menial tasks like fetching water and waiting at table. He dined off the remains of the food from the Fellows' tables thus obtaining his 'sizings' or extra delicacies without paying for them. The custom continued at Trinity until as recently as 1840.

Pensioner .... Term formerly used for the main body of undergraduates who paid normal fees for their tuition and board.

Proctors .... Principal disciplinary officers of the University. The office dates back to the early fourteenth century and gives the Proctors many rights, including those of entering licensed premises and places of public entertainment. Their authority does not extend inside a college, but college authorities will nearly always take some form of action on a Proctor's report.

Bulldogs .... Each Proctor is usually accompanied by two henchmen or 'bulldogs' drawn from the more stalwart examples of college servants. Fleetness of foot is a worthwhile attribute should an undergraduate stopped by a Proctor decide to make a dash for it.

Esquire Bedells .... Originally three in number but now two, they are graduate members of the university whose duty is to attend the Chancellor or Vice Chancellor on public occasions. They can be distinguished by the fine silver maces they carry, presented to the University by the Duke of Buckingham when Chancellor in 1626.

Bedders .... Bedmakers who also clean, wash up and generally attend upon Fellows and undergraduates living in college. First employed from the eighteenth century on..ards when they took over the duties from the sizars or poor students. Bedders are by tradition women of the town who at one time were chosen for their married status and lack of looks in an effort to preserve undergraduate morals. These days bedders can be single and attractive.

Gyps .... A vanishing race of college menservants who these days attend mainly upon Fellows. 'Gypping', like bed-making, ran in families who established themselves as integral parts of college life.

Gyp room .... Pantries on various college staircases formerly used by the gyps but now much used by the undergraduates themselves for tea and coffee making.

King's College main entrance and Chapel with the Senate House, St John's tower and the Waterhouse building of Gonville and Caius also visible.

INDEX

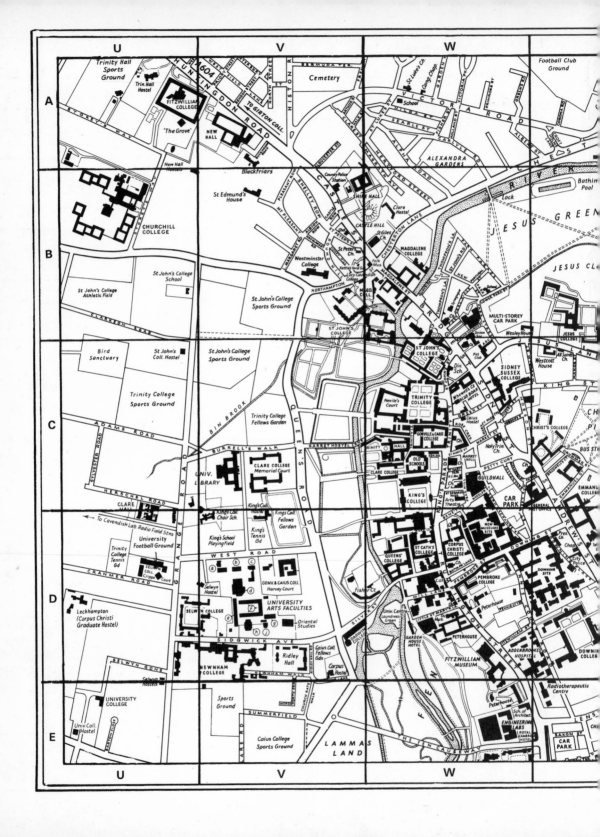